MORE OFF CENTER:

A PEEK INTO THE PAST

by
HELEN MACLENNAN RAMBOW

ILLUSTRATIONS
by
JEAN DENNIS DIX
and
JONATHAN H.C. RAMBOW

Dedicated to
CAMILLA and HARRY

Also author of:
Jo Mendi — His Life and Antics
Off Center
Chattermarks
The It of It

ISBN 0-9613687-0-5

TABLE OF CONTENTS

"And the eagle
Will tell it to its young,
    And pine to pine
And the winds, in the dark recesses,
Shall whisper our many fond memories."

—GLENN R. ALEXANDER

PRESS NOTICES

Mrs. May Stocking Knaggs, of Bay City, chairman of the Press Committee for the Woman's Convention (National Woman's Relief Corps), is a New York woman of New England descent, resident for the last twenty years in Michigan, educator, writer, artist, orator and charming woman. * * * A logical and convincing speaker, she has been of great service in awaking popular and legislative thought on the subject of equal suffrage.—*Detroit Free Press.*

Mrs. May S. Knaggs, of Bay City, Mich, was a guest of the convention, and was presented by Miss Susan B. Anthony. Mrs. Knaggs is a pleasing woman, a gifted and fluent speaker.—*Auburn (N. Y.) Bulletin.*

The union temperance meeting Sunday evening was largely attended. Mrs. Knaggs gave a very pleasing address. * * * She is moderate in her language, and at all times impresses the audience as a refined and sincere lady.

Mrs. Knaggs gave her lecture on Woman's Right to Citizenship at the M. E. church, Monday evening, to a fair-sized audience.

She is very fair in all her arguments and accurate in her statements. She meets the principal objections to woman's right to vote with convincing logic and facts.—*Butler Co. News, Shell Rock, Iowa.*

Mrs. Knaggs followed Miss Anthony, and gave a very clear history of the municipal suffrage law. She is a ready speaker and at once interests her hearers.—*Washtenaw Evening Times, Ann Arbor, Mich.*

The women of Warsaw are indebted to the Political Equality Club for a rare treat in a free lecture given by Mrs. May Stocking Knaggs, of Michigan, on Friday afternoon. Mrs. Knaggs has an interesting personality, and is an earnest and effective speaker.—*Wyoming County (N. Y.) Times.*

The Political Equality Club gave the public a rare treat last Friday, in a free lecture by Mrs. May S. Knaggs, of Michigan. Mrs. Knaggs has a charming personality, and speaks in a delightfully easy, cultivated manner. Her points are all well taken and effective.—*Western New-Yorker, Warsaw, N. Y.*

The lecture given in the Army Post room last Saturday evening, by Mrs. May Stocking Knaggs, on the subject of Political Equality, was the finest woman suffrage lecture we ever listened to in any place. Its clear, calm reasoning, its just and careful statements, its earnest yet kindly spirit, as well as the winsome yet dignified manner of its delivery, cannot be too highly commended. The speaker has a very magnetic personality. Every point she made bristled with argument, fact and statistics, and the whole lecture was pervaded with a sweet, kindly spirit toward men.—*The Suffolk Weekly Times, Greenport, N.Y.*

The W. C. T. U., as a body, have with great unanimity, reached the mile-stone of "equal suffrage" in their march of progress, and one of their brightest members, Mrs. May S. Knaggs, of Bay City, discussed this subject with all its complicated bearings, on Wednesday evening, to a crowded house, which opportunely contained quite a large sprinkling of the "present voter." She handled her subject with skill, delicacy, and intelligence, and with such a kindly spirit that even those who differed with her respected the cause and its advocate.—*Tuscola Co. Pioneer, Vassar, Mich.*

Several hundred ladies and a few brave men attended the equal suffrage meeting held in the Auditorium at 2 o'clock yesterday afternoon. Mrs. Judge Andrew Howell, of Detroit presided.

The speaker of the hour was Mrs. May S. Knaggs, president of the Equal Suffrage Association of Michigan, who is a forcible and pleasing speaker. Her address was a logical presentation of the claims of the cause, and it was delivered in a manner that was calculated to secure and hold the attention and to convince the hearer.—*The Daily Resorter, Petoskey, Mich. Bay View Assembly Notes.*

Two meetings were held last week to advocate equal suffrage: one in West-Hampton Beach Friday evening, and the other Saturday evening in the West-Hampton M. E. church. The speaker was Mrs. May Stocking Knaggs, of Bay City, Michigan; certainly a very gifted woman, clear and logical in her style of thought, and exceedingly modest and pleasing in the presentation of her subject.

On Sunday afternoon Mrs. Knaggs also addressed the Quogue Colored Mission, on the life and work of Christ. In every case this Michigan orator speaks to edification, winning and holding the attention of her audience and gaining friends for the cause she advocates.—*Sag-Harbor (N. Y.) Express*

Mrs. May Stocking Knaggs gave a telling speech for equal suffrage in the school-house at Ghent, Saturday evening. She comes from Michigan and this was the fifty-first lecture she has given in this state campaign.—*Chatham (N. Y.) Courier.*

OFF CENTER (1884–1920)

"Home is where we tie one end of the thread of life."
-The Warm World of Martin Busbaum
(Acropolis Books Ltd.)

Bay City

Reared just off Center Street in Bay City, Michigan, our Father and Mother lived across the street from each other in childhood, youth, and young adulthood, sweethearts forever.

Down through the years, laughing until we cried in idiot's delight over each new episode of our crazy crew, we point to the sheer simplicity of our origin — just off Center.

Center Street now is one of the most architecturally significant streets in the United States. Just off Center, in 1884 Gram and Gramp built a house of many wonders.

It did not sport a ballroom as did many of the three-story homes built by lumbermen on Center. Now, 100 years later, it still is a handsome house of Queen Anne persuasion.

Lowest, but most important to us, was the basement. Chief mechanical wonder here was the toilet seat made to rise with the sitter and automatically flush. We, alas, were too light in weight for it and often found ourselves the risen before we were ready.

The door leading from the toilet to the laundry room never did have a knob or handle, but instead was adorned with an old rope that had become frayed through the years. Just as big sister Marion could hold up a nail and say, "Helen, this is a worm" and my imagination would send me screaming around the house, so the old rope became a cow's tail.

By grasping the cow's tail, with one swift swoop I could emerge from the toilet seat and out of the room which was dark and always a little scary, anyway, and be well on my way.

We loved to tinker and Gramp's workshop was always open, if grudgingly, to the children. At least we always felt welcome to take over, entering by a front basement window as the preferred route. There we made ships to sail the seven seas out of bits of wood, spools, nails, and string.

In the stall in the basement reigned the rickshaw, handsome thing of regal glory. Rubber-tired, wicker-seated, and softly cushioned, it was something we all dearly loved to ride in. With all pomp and circumstance it was hitched to Gramp's bike and off we'd go, the proudest children in the city.

Bay City was a bicycle manufacturing city, and this was the ultra in bicycle attachments. Even the electric auto at Gates' house next door never had anything on Gramp's rickshaw, as far as we were concerned.

City water, for some reason, was considered unfit for consumption and we bought spring water in huge jars which had to be siphoned out into smaller jars. I was urged to learn how to siphon, but I worried about spiders emerging from the rubber tubing into my mouth during this basement chore.

Big stalks with many bunches of bananas were hung in the basement which we took as a great opportunity to invite neighborhood kids to share with us.

The rear basement doors were opened by pulling on huge rocks dangling in wire. These doors made marvelous slides in winter.

Hurrying through the front door of the house when we entered more decorously, we would rush past a big heavy halltree and a small pedestal for calling cards left by visitors on days "at home."

The parlor was one to remember, especially with its beloved piano on which Gram without fail played the Doxology each Sunday morning before breakfast.

Evenings Gram and Gramp sat there together in the twilight, with the leaves of the apple trees tracing a miraculous flickering pattern on the floor and walls. We sat, too, in the spell of the dusk, until it was really dark. Then Gramp would flick on the lights. (We later were told that his was the first residence in Bay City to boast electricity.) Gramp, having only one arm, would read his evening paper held up on a reading stick, such as librarians use, thus easily holding and handling his paper.

In the sitting room stood the large, round library table covered with a heavily fringed shawl. On the table was a basket holding recent mail, the latest letter from each person writ-

ing being retained until another replaced it. (There never was a "last letter" until the writer died.)

A stereoptican viewer and slides invited the curious, and many papers and journals, including "Little Folks" and "St. Nicholas" intrigued our interest. Nearby on a metal stand was a large dictionary. Floor to ceiling bookcases lined one wall on the shelves of which were tiny monks perched at our eye level though not to be touched. The room was warmed by a big burner with isinglass windows revealing rosy coals within.

The alcove off the sitting room was a place of mystery and heroic deed. It was ideal as a stage and many's the time we enacted Washington Crossing the Delaware, played charades, or gave shadow pictures or some other skit, just as our parents had done before us.

The "stage" was heavily curtained. Its backdrop was an oil painting of my Uncle Roy as a child of nine or ten. The fascinating thing about this portrait was the fact that someone had at some time taken aim and shot out all the buttons on his suit.

There was much conjecture, when we grew up, about who did this dastardly deed, a jealous sibling or just boys at play? We never knew.

Gram's rolltop desk presided in the alcove and was a treasure trove of spindles, clips, ticket punchers, and a circular Franklin typewriter. Either she was too busy to notice, didn't

"Ready aim fire!"

mind too much, or gave up in despair, but we carried on full business careers fiendishly in our play.

The closet in the alcove was surreptitiously visited all too frequently by the grandchildren who found "hidden" there hundreds of chocolate "pennies" and sheets of three-layered candy.

Gramp satisfied his grandchildren's collective sweet tooth by fussing with candy-making in the kitchen. He would spread an immense counter-wide layer of bitter chocolate covered by a layer of luscious fondant topped by a layer of sweet chocolate.

We never had to check on "what's for dinner" or, more important, "what's for dessert" from outside the house as the pantry sported a screened shelf outside its one window where puddings or pies were cooled. We could see and smell but not touch. How fragrant the tastes and smells of childhood — and how keen even today is the remembered combined odor of washday and cooking cabbage which assailed our nostrils on Mondays at Gramp's house.

I'm sure we made the act of stair climbing one of sheer torture for our grandparents. We jumped from ever higher successive bare stairs to the landing, our great hope being to jump the whole flight at once some day.

In the upper hallway stood a horsehair trunk the contents of which remained forever an unsolved mystery.

Upstairs the then newly installed bathroom was a place for lingering — where we acquainted ourselves with the playing figures in the Kate Greenaway wallpaper. On an antique highboy perched a stuffed owl and under a tall glass dome delicate coral was on display. On the wall hung a calendar depicting Sherman's dramatic March to the Sea.

Camilla, age 7, and doll Pansy

Off Gram's and Gramp's bedroom with its bay and corner windows was a closet in which skulked a menacing, forever-ticking meter. Closely associated in our minds when hiding there was a picture of the sphinx on the opposite wall.

In the front bedroom, which was usually ours when we visited or lived there, we remember particularly the deep shadows of the leafy trees that made the room a mysteriously moving, bobbing place until sleep overtook us.

Just off the bedroom was the washroom with an oval window. Soft water always awaited in the china pitcher and the prized Pear's soap Gram indulged in for her guests. The fragrance of Pear's soap and witch hazel for all bumps and bruises is inextricably interwoven in our childhood memories of a Mercurechromeless world — balm for any wound.

In this little room on its side rested the swan tin tub we begged to be bathed in long after installation of the claw and ball tub in the bathroom. Cousin Carol remembers a bath in the sitting room downstairs in front of the big burner. We used the swan tub as a special treat long after we were too big for it, lopping over most ungracefully.

The third bedroom housed the childhood doll trunks of Mother and Aunt Mary. We played with the self-same china-faced Violet and Pansy they played with. These dolls were beautifully dressed even to high-button shoes.

A Hundred Years Ago

New men and methods, systems, creeds,
　New fabrics, nostrums, wares,
Arise and pass as years roll by,
　Yet there's no change in PEAR'S;
With princes and with cottagers,
　With artisans and peers,
It's been the toilet favorite
　Over a hundred years.

The beauties of the ancient days
　Of powder, puff, and patch,
Kept faithful to their faithful PEARS,
　And never found its match;
And when the aged century
　Dies out and disappears,
PEARS' SOAP will still be foremost
　Another hundred years.

(From the Easter 1895 edition of Munsey's
Magazine)

The maid's room housed a succession of maids, the most elegant of which was Rose. Rose wore big "picture" hats, thin veils, starched "fronts" and skirts. We always were called to the parlor when a former maid came to call, so she could see how her former charges had grown.

Those were the days of color and flamboyancy. Bay City will forever mean to us the Knights Templar in their plumed hats parading down Center Street or pacing the slow measures of the Dead March from Saul; the streets named for the Presidents; the awe-inspiring fire-wagon drawn by a dashing team of four horses, the ladders swinging from side to side; the barn a block away with a carriage turn-table which became our merry-go-round. All this we saw from "our" backyard — and more.

Still quite small, hand in hand, sister Marion and I would venture down to Water Street to buy penny dolls (ten dolls for one cent to kill as Indians), peeking under the swinging saloon doors at the high boots of lumbermen within.

On the way home we paused in the park to inspect the cannon and huge cannon balls, and perhaps stop at the drug store for that heavenly dish, a sarsaparilla soda.

On other days we were sent with small gifts to the Old Ladies Home. There we saw Aunt Mary Doe (one of the early presidents of the Michigan Equal Suffrage Association formed in 1884). She always had peppermints in the pocket of her apron. We also visited with Aunty Rathburn who was over 90 years of age and read her Bible through its entirety every year.

There was one palsied resident to whom we took a tin pail of freshly picked cherries. How fascinated we were when her pathetic palsied hand rattled in the pail as she removed the ripe red fruit! Wickedly, we later practiced to see who could best imitate her infirmity.

Coming home, we would travel up Fifth Avenue, which was the next street parallel to Center, picking at the hot tar between the round wooden blocks that paved this thorough-fare (fine substitute for today's chewing gum).

As we turned off Fifth Avenue onto Sheridan, where we lived in the middle of the three-house block, it was always a race to the first of the two owl hitching posts in front of the house. These twin posts had owl heads perched on top. All game losers' penalties consisted of wiping out the cobwebs from the owls' brains (horrid task).

Almost every house on Center had its third story ball-room. We, as the spoiled third generation, roller-skated and swooped and slid about these hardwood polished floors.

The Gates' house next door was always, to us, a mansion of mystery and charm. A great wide stairway led to the second floor, and a narrower stairway to a birds-eye maple ballroom. A third spiral stairway was for servants only.

The formal drawing room was done in white and the chairs were gilt. In the upstairs "sitting-room," which was papered with red cabbage roses, were a grand piano and a beautiful fireplace before which the women of the household sometimes hoisted their skirts as they stood warming themselves in winter.

Grandma Gates had a penetrating, rather strident voice, and we could hear her call to her daughter, "Gertrude, Gertrude" and their parrot mock her raucously, "GER-trude, GER-trude."

Mrs. Gates' electric car often stood in the porte-cochere. Even a vase with flowers graced one corner of the car's black interior. I particularly remember how quietly it ran.

"Gone are the days" and delights of Off Center, but how wonderful to "remember the time when."

THERE'S A RAISIN

Gramp (1839–1925)

"One anecdote of a man is worth a volume of biography."
—*William Ellery Channing*

Gramp's — and our — first ancestor to this country helped settle Detroit. He was George Knaggs, 1st, who came to the Maumee Valley in 1760 from England. His mother was a native of Wales. He married Rachel Sly, a native of the Mohawk Valley, N.Y., and of Holland Dutch extraction.

A new settlement called Fort Pontchartrain (later Detroit) was established in 1701 by Antoine de la Mothe Cadillac. There were 250,000 inhabitants in the colonies at that time.

In 1760 Detroit was surrendered by the French Commander Beletre to the British under the command of Major Robert Rogers.

Surrounded by Indians, George and Rachel engaged in barter with them. So in 1768 George, with three other men, bought a lot 45 × 42 feet on St. Anne St. at the corner of Campau alley in Detroit. The lot was located about the center of the present Jefferson Ave. and 200 feet west of Griswold St.

At this time Benjamin Franklin had already invented the Franklin stove (1742) and the first wallpaper had been sold (1730).

George and Rachel had eight children, all born on the Maumee River and educated at home by their mother in Latin and Dutch as well as in the elementary branches of education. They were baptized at the Huron Jesuit mission at Sandwich, Ont. George was a Protestant or *indifferentist*, but his wife was a strict Catholic and the children were reared in that faith.

What a term, indifferentist. That is what so many people are today.

Our great great grandfather, James, son of George 1st., was their sixth child. His brother, Whitmore, was adopted by the Ottawa Indians as a member of their nation which, as a token of love and affection, subsequently deeded him a tract of land consisting of 3,864 acres on the Maumee in 1784, eight years after the signing of the Declaration of Independence. A part of this later was the site of Fort Miami.

Whitmore later became attached to Mad Anthony Wayne's Army as scout and interpreter of Indian tongues. During the Battle of Fallen Timbers in 1794, Whitmore's younger brother, James, then only 14, was also a scout and soldier.

George Knaggs' trading post at Maumee was destroyed by Wayne's troops and he took refuge in Fort Miami. Finally, Fort Miami and Fort Lernoult at Detroit were evacuated by the British and occupied by American troops under the command of Colonel John Francis Hamtramck on July 11, 1796, during Washington's last year as President. (Colonel Hamtramck is the man for whom Hamtramck, MI is named.)

In 1800 the colony's population was 5,368,483 and there were 896,849 slaves. John Chapman spread the Johnny Appleseed legend throughout the Ohio Valley along with the Gospel.

After George Knaggs 1st.'s death in 1809, Rachel Knaggs was granted 259 acres on the north side of the Raisin River. My grandmother (May Stocking Knaggs) had in her possession, a parchment bearing the signatures of James Madison, President, and James Monroe, Secretary of State, dated May 30, 1811, for this tract of land.

In 1812 whites were driven out of the Lake Michigan area by Indians in the Ft. Dearborn massacre.

When Rachel was 80 years old, she went through a harrowing experience. After the battle of the Raisin in 1813, she hid a citizen, whose life was threatened by the Indians, under a hogshead. General Proctor, who had permitted the Indians to massacre the Kentucky prisoners, ordered her to leave town. He commanded her to go to Detroit.

According to the historian Lossing, "Thinly clad, having been robbed by the Indians, she proceeded to Detroit in bitter cold in an open traineau. . . . When asked how it happened she did not freeze, she replied, 'My spunk kept me warm.'

"She subsequently returned to her farm on the River Raisin, seven miles from Frenchtown, now known as Monroe, MI."

James, my great, great grandfather, was a staunch patriot. A veritable Hercules in size, he is described as active as "a wildcat, upright as a dart." His teeth were a curiosity, being double. A swift runner, champion wrestler, and excelling in woodcraft, in war he was described as "crafty, acute, courageous, resourceful, and audacious. In manner he was fond of humorous sayings and anecdotes. He was a democrat and a Presbyterian."

In the Michigan Pioneer Collection of 1890, my grandmother recalled that James Knaggs, while operating a ferry across the Huron River, foiled an assault by Indians he was taking across. He managed to knock one into the water with a paddle and held him under until half drowned. The Indian was so grateful not to be killed he later presented a brightly colored handkerchief to James.

James Knaggs once killed two Indians who came to kill him. They shot directly at him at short range but missed. He managed to close his front door and run to a rear window and climb out. The Indians chased him around the house. On the third time around he grabbed a hoe, turned on them, and killed them.

An Indian chief, father of one, came to kill him in revenge. He carried a gun across his saddle and said, "You killed my son." But James took away his gun.

Later he was taken prisoner by the Indians and they decided to burn him at the stake. He lay bound in a tepee all night. At dawn he was carried out and placed upright against a tall tree. As they piled resinous wood around him he was approached by an old squaw, mother of one of the Indians he had slain. She put a belt of wampum around James' neck, caressed him, and said, "You are my son." Since this was the equivalent of adoption, the men, though angered, could not kill him. He was given a horse, saddle, and bridle, and set free.

James Knaggs was one of eight men who notified Commodore Perry on his ship in Lake Erie that the people of Detroit wanted him to come there as soon as possible. In 1812–13 the people of Detroit were virtual prisoners of the British. Perry promised to bring his ships by morning and asked the eight men to pilot him by their canoe.

A cousin of our great grandfather, George Knaggs, was a son of George B. Knaggs, and an Indian named Kah-ba-yan-no-qua. He, in turn, at 20 married an Indian Now-quash-kum-mo-qua and lived on Walpole Island. They had two children. He and his second wife, Ke-wa-tin, had three children. I recall that the name of a passenger boat on the Great Lakes was Kewatin. It is now moored and on display at Muskegon, MI.

Due to these stories about our family's connection with Indians, my sister Marion and I for years deluded ourselves into believing we were descended from Indian princesses, no less. That explained our long, black straight hair, we thought.

However, my mother, Camilla, did come across one of the Walpole Indian descendents when working at the Protestant Children's Home in Detroit. A young man, orphaned, who had grown up there, had become an artist. His name was Edwin Knaggs.

Gramp with grand-daughter Marion

A native of Monroe and one of 10 children and oldest son of Johnson Knaggs, son of James, Gramp (John Wesley Knaggs) enlisted soon after the Civil War broke out. He never could talk to his children about his experiences but he told us, his grandchildren. A private in Company A, Fourth Michigan Infantry, he fought in the seven-day battle ending in the Battle of Malvern Hill July 1, 1862, where retreating Union forces under General McClellan repulsed the Confederates under General Lee. He lost his left arm after lying for seven days upon the battlefield. Taken prisoner by the Confederates, his arm was amputated at Libby Prison without benefit of anesthesia as they "had none to spare on the enemy."

After one month he was exchanged and taken to Bellevue Hospital, New York, where he remained six months. He told us that fighting off the flies was the worst of his experiences and showed us the knife, fork and spoon he used in the Army as well as the strainer through which he strained water from mud puddles and ditches for drinking. Due to his Civil War service he later in life became a member and commander of H.P.Merrill Post No. 419, GAR.

All his life, Gramp managed to do everything anyone else could do and never asked for help. At the table he had a rubber mat beside his plate so he could cut his own meat with one hand.

After the Civil War ended, Gramp returned to Monroe, MI where he worked as a bookkeeper. I always wondered how my grandmother from Spring Lake, N.Y. and Gramp got together. I was 77 before I found out. It seems that her father, my great grandfather, Dr. Charles Giles Stocking, practiced medicine in Monroe one year, returning to Spring Lake. Gram must have lived there too during that time, thus meeting Gramp.

Upon moving to Bay City in 1865, Gramp engaged in the insurance business, the firm being Knaggs and Denison, and in 1881 Knaggs, Clark and Plum. The century-old partnership still survives as the Plum Agency under the guidance of Paul R. Ryden.

Gramp loved trees and birds and hated cats. He delighted in grafting trees. Some of his combinations would have done credit to a Burbank. He had early and late apples on the same tree, making a constant parade of fruit. Apricot trees bore peaches and he even grafted pansies on hollyhock stalks! He made us eat apples, core, seeds and all, saying it was all good for us.

Attempts were made to save his prize fruit from bruising by spreading canvas through the trees to catch them, or at least to break their fall. He later invented a fruit snipper with basket attached. He thoroughly believed in no organic waste and replenished his garden with the family garbage. A standing family joke was "he's out burying his nephews," meaning refuse.

One of Gramp's many inventions was a vacuum sweeper with the outlet down through each floor, so that the dirt would be conveyed directly to the basement, a forerunner of today's gadgets.

Harrison Plum, grandson of Gramp's insurance partner, Allen G. Plum, tells us Gramp had difficulty managing the usual snowplow or shovel with his one arm so he invented a plow that he could steer with one hand and push with his chest on a bar-piece inserted from handle to handle.

Harrison also tells this story about Gramp: It seems he came home to a locked house, no one home, and no key in his possession. Always independent and resourceful, he got his ladder and placed it at the one upstairs window he knew to be unlocked. He climbed up, crawled in, locked the window, went downstairs and opened the front door, returned to the ladder and put it away.

Just then, he heard the front door blow shut.

He returned to the ladder and searched each upper window for one unlocked. Finding one, he started to climb in but slipped and fell to the ground, breaking his one good arm.

Gramp once was awakened by a burglar's hand rattling in a "button dish" on their bureau. He sat up in bed and let out a "Comanche war-whoop". The burglar was so frightened he fell down the stairway, stabbing himself with scissors he was carrying, and ran out of the house, leaving a trail of blood.

A Russell-ite, Gramp believed that the Golden Millenium was at hand and that "millions now living will never die." He thought he could prophesy World War I from the Bible and also the end of the world.

He used to say emphatically, "The trumpet will blow on the Day of Judgment and all those who believe will rise."

Grandma Knaggs answered firmly, "Wesley, when the trumpet blows, *I* shall not arise."

Gramp was a graduate of Albion College. From the days of Lincoln he identified with the Republican party. Active in advancing the interests of Bay City, he was one of a company of six capitalists who started the first sugar beet factory in the city in 1866.

When a small child, I was taken by Gramp to see the beet sugar mills. When we left, I was given a little box of sugar which I carefully kept in my bureau drawer. Every once in a while I'd open the drawer, moisten my forefinger and stick it in the sugar and lick it off. That was the most delicious sweet I have ever known — my own secret supply — in spite of the fact that I'm sure I remember seeing men walk all over the sugar at the mill.

The sugar beet seeds came from Germany and France. The Cuban reciprocity treaty placed such a low tariff on Cuban cane sugar it "did in" the beet sugar business.

Grandpa took us to Wenonah Park where I can remember going through the tunnel of love. I can remember the thousands of Mayflies that descended on the park each Spring. I recall being told that they lived only for a day.

A lemon tree in a big wooden tub graced the dining room at Gramp's house. He drank a large bowl of hot fresh lemon juice half an hour before breakfast each day. He lived to a "ripe old age" and 'tis said he died from eating too much citrus fruit after going to Florida with his second wife, Belle M., and starting a fruit farm at St. Petersburg after he was 80. He died there in 1925 at 85.

Growing up along the River Raisin, "There's a raisin" became a family slogan for Gramp and his siblings. There was one brother, Freedom, whose name I thought was most romantic. And there was my great uncle Dan, whose son, Daniel Knaggs, became the famous Mayor of Monroe who stood up so sturdily against strikers and for man's "right to work."

Cousin Jim Stone preserved the following letter written by my Uncle Roy to his cousin Daniel:
. . . . . . "Now that you have had the spotlight of publicity turned upon you and you have so sensibly carried on in the face of great odds, I want to congratulate and applaud you, for it sends chills rippling along my backbone to find in you the determination and ability latent in the Knaggs clan. Your father before you and your grandfather John and your great grandfather James Knaggs the Indian fighter, all exhibited these characteristics reflected in you and all were on the side of law and order.

". . . . . I have many pleasant boyhood pictures

of Monroe as we children used to vacation on grandfather's farm every summer.

"I believe it was before your time, but Grandfather Stocking (mother's father) was a practicing physician in Monroe for a time, living on the East side of the river bank above the convent when I was a little kid. He finally returned to New York State, but we children divided our visits with both grandparents, much to the annoyance of the maternal side, Grandma Knaggs, Aunt Myra and Uncle Bryant.

"My mother's sister, Aunt 'Nim' (Mrs. C. H. Denison) living here (New York City) in her 85th year and quite active, asks me to tell you that she 'commends your courage' and declares 'you are one of the few real Americans left.' "

Great Uncle Bryant and his sister, Myra, eked out their frugal existence through life together, saving, saving for that day of need. They boasted that they shared an egg a day for ten years, and it is said that Great Aunt Myra's forefinger was permanently bent backward from getting that last drop out of the bowl.

All their frugality went for naught. Uncle Bryant married a sweet young thing in his middle age. Six months after the honeymoon they both were struck by a train at a crossing and killed. The bride lived a trifle longer than Uncle Bryant. Her family inherited the lifetime "wealth". Poor Aunt Myra learned sorrowfully the errors of her egg eking.

The moral: Eat one whole egg a day.

May Stocking Knaggs, who served as president of the Michigan State Equal Suffrage Association for four years.

Gram (1847–1917)

"It were indeed a desirable thing to be well descended, but the glory thereof belongs to our ancestors."
— Plutarch

Gram (May Stocking Knaggs), mother of four, Roy, Walter, Camilla and Mary, was an ardent woman suffragist, a brilliant public speaker, prolific writer, and a hob-nobber with such women as Carrie Chapman Catt, Elizabeth Cady Stanton, and Susan B. Anthony. She also was a poet and an artist.

When Gram's famous friends came to visit her, I sat in a corner and ogled them, worrying about their eyes, which seemed to me so deepset they might fall back into their heads, like my doll's eyes did once.

The story goes that the quietly attired Susan B. Anthony would precede Elizabeth Cady Stanton to town and make all the important contacts and arrangements for rallies, then Elizabeth would sweep into town like a queen. Of course it is the modest Susan who has received all the accolades "as time goes by."

Leaving her patient and admiring husband at home with the children, Gram went barnstorming around the country on ever new and uplifting projects in the name of suffrage. Gramp would see Gram off at the train with the baby carriage and toddlers and happily meet her again upon her return from each such trip. They understood each other.

Gram served as a guardian of the Michigan Industrial Home for Girls, Adrian, and as a member of the board of the Home of Industry for Discharged Prisoners at Detroit by appointment by Governor Bliss. She was one of the first women to serve on the Board of Education in Bay City.

Neither Delay Nor Rest

Gram served as president of the State Equal Suffrage Association for four years under Susan B. Anthony. Found under the floorboards of her attic almost 100 years later by Miss Patricia Drury, present owner, were letters from the National American Women's Suffrage Association, the slogan of which at that time was "Neither Delay Nor Rest." Also found was a report of the 6th Annual Convention of the Michigan Equal Suffrage Association held in Detroit Feb. 13 and 14, 1890, and a program of the 12th Annual Convention in Pontiac May 20, 21, and 22, 1896, at which time Gram gave the president's address.

The March 6, 1887 issue of the Bay City Tribune reported on Mrs. J. W. Knaggs' (Gram's) "irresistible argument why women should be given the right of suffrage" after being introduced by Frances E. Willard to the joint committees of the Michigan Senate Judiciary and House committee in behalf of a bill granting equal suffrage to women.

"After preparing my address for this occasion I was painfully aware that it consisted only of arguments which have been presented again and again. For in the nearly forty years during which woman has been asking for suffrage everything has been said in its favor which is in any way possible. . . . We are very weary of saying these things over and over. We hope that this is the last time we shall be required to do it. That the bill before the legislature will become a law. If it happens that it does not it does not follow that we will give the matter up, but we shall certainly come again and again if necessary, until the measure prevails," she began.

Accused of being "merely" a reformer, Gram fought back.

"Do I want to be a reformer? To decide the question I let my mind run back over the history of the past to that epoch when the name first became prominent. To the reformation when Martin Luther stood up in the eyes of the world and threw off the papal fetters from the mind and soul. Further down the page comes Oliver Cromwell, whose life was spent in efforts to establish a form of government which was the forerunner of our own republic. A little farther down George Washington, 'the defender of liberty, the friend of man.' Then again down the page, Abraham Lincoln, who struck the shackles from the hands of four million slaves and lifted from us the shadow of a great national crime. And around and between the central suns upon the pages of history cluster galaxies of brilliant names of men and women.

"And now my name, hitherto obscure and unknown, is added to the glorious list. And, gentlemen, if the exceeding effulgence of this brilliant array shall still render it obscure, it is there, and I shall thank the honorable gentleman for the unspeakable honor he has conferred upon me.

"We come before you asking 'municipal suffrage for the women citizens of Michigan.' . . . "In our state at the present time there are over a million and a half of 'the people.' Of these nearly one half are under the age entitling them to exercise the rights of citizenship. Of the remainder nearly one half are women, who by reason of their sex have never been included under the first definition of citizens. . . . Therefore the will of the majority of one-fourth of the people of Michigan is represented in the governing power. We find that in every other respect women are regarded as citizens. A woman can and many do take active part in the business of the community. She can buy, sell, maintain herself and family, accumulate and hold property.

"Every intelligent man and woman who has traced the history of mankind knows that woman has come by slow degrees from a low condition of serfdom. That when man was savage, woman was a slave. That brute force made right in every relation. That in proportion as man has become civilized the shackles have been taken from the hands and feet of woman and that she has never abused her growing liberty. In our free country of America, to the credit of its men be it said, she has attained unparalleled freedom.

"It is now nearly 39 years since women first publicly 'Resolved, that it is the duty of the women of this country to secure to themselves their sacred right to the elective franchise.' During subsequent years of effort to fulfill that duty women have been repeatedly met with the statement that they are already represented by fathers, brothers and husbands. What a paradox! Virtually represented, then. But, said the great Pitt, with reference to the American colonies: 'The idea of virtual representation is the most contemptible that ever entered into the head of man. It does not deserve a serious refutation.'

"We arrive, then, at the bottom fact, that the women of our state are unrepresented in its government. We petition your honorable committee to report favorably to the assembled legislature upon a bill to 'secure to the women of Michigan the right to vote in the election of all town and city officers and upon all local questions because, first, property-holding women are taxed without representation, which was one of the prime reasons for our declaration of independence of Great Britain, the 'imposing of taxes on us without our consent.' Second, the interests of man and woman are identical. The city is made up of homes. In the home the interests of the father and mother, of the man and woman, are identical. . . .

"There is no difference of sex in intellect. A woman solves a quadratic equation by the same process of reasoning as a man. 'When the rivet falls from a pair of scissors we do not have them mended because either half can claim superiority over the other half, but because it takes two halves to make a whole.'

"The laws of the state of Michigan, we are aware, are largely in favor of women. We recognize the chivalry which prompted these laws. But what women want in this age of the world is not chivalry but justice."

"The woman's cause is man's; they rise and sink
Together, dwarfed or god-like, bond or free,
If she be small, slight-natured, miserable,
How shall men grow?
. . . . . As far as in us lies,
We then will serve them both in aiding her.
Will clear away the parasitic forms,
That seem to keep her up, but drag her down.
Will leave her space to burgeon out of all
Within her, let her make herself her own,
To give or keep, and live and learn, and be
All that not harms distinctive womanhood.
Yet in the long years liker must they grow.
The man be more of woman, she of man:
He gain in sweetness and in moral height,
She mental breadth, nor fail in childward care,
Till at the last she set herself to man,
Like perfect music unto noble words,
And so these twain upon the skirts of time
Sit side by side, full summed in all their powers.
Then comes the statelier Eden back to man:
Then reign the world's great bridals chaste and calm:
Then springs the crowning race of humankind.
May these things be."

Born Mariette (May) Stocking December 14, 1847, Gram was the daughter of Dr. and Mrs. Charles G. Stocking (Mary Woodhull). They lived in Penn Yan, Seneca Falls, Montezuma, Westburg, and Spring Lake, N.Y., and for a short time in Monroe, MI.

The Stocking ancestry reaches back to the early settlement of New England. About one million Indians lived in North

America when European exploration began. In 1602 the first Englishman landed in New England and named the place Cape Cod.

In 1607 John Smith was saved from the Indians by Pocohontas, daughter of Chief Powhatan. In 1608 he was taught how to raise Indian corn by two Indians. In the same year John Robinson's Separatist or Independent community became the nucleus of the colonists who sailed to America on the Mayflower and founded Plymouth. The pilgrims on the 63-day voyage numbered 41 men and their families.

The year 1612 saw the beginnings of New York City and in 1626 the "Manhattes" Island was sold by the Indians for 60 guilders, or $24.

On November 11, 1620 the Mayflower compact became the basis of government for the New England colonies, drafted and signed by the 41 adult males in Provincetown Harbor. On December 21 the pilgrims arrived. Miles Standish was appointed the first military officer in the colonies. Dr. Samuel Fuller was the first physician to serve the New England colony. By 1629 the colonial population rose to 2,499.

First in the Stocking family to arrive in America was George Stocking in 1633. He and his wife and four children sailed across the ocean on the ship Griffin. After the death of his first wife, Anna, he married Agnes Shotwell Webster, the widow of John Webster, governor of the colony, and lived to be 101.

George Stocking's son, Deacon Samuel Stocking, married Bethia Hopkins, granddaughter of one of the signers of the "Mayflower Compact" in 1620.

So Gram came by her interest in public affairs naturally and took her place in intellectual reform and philanthropic movements "with masculine strength of mind," to quote the

"History of Bay County." She was active in the first opportunity for women to vote in Bay County, MI.

She and Gramp were married June 9, 1864. Gram died in New York City in 1917 and was buried at Kensico Cemetery.

As their children grew up, Gram insisted that they each contribute to the family monthly paper MINCE PIE and periodically she invited the local editor to come to the house and enjoy a "reading" of it. The children often protested but their efforts to hone their creative talents I'm sure resulted in greater writing abilities and inventiveness.

Gram was an inveterate letter writer and her children followed suit. Found under the floorboards of the attic of their home when it was 100 years old was one written on birch bark from her son, Roy, who sailed to the Les Chenaux Islands and survived being capsized when rescued by an Indian. The letter:

Les Cheneaux
July 30, 1892

Dear Mother

I don't know whether I can't fill this sheet or not. We went after raspberries yesterday afternoon and George and I together picked four quarts. I hope this wind does not blow so hard tomorrow as it does today for we want to go tomorrow. I did not have time to thank Mrs. Bassett nor M. Piiz for you as I only had time to read your letter and write a postal before leaving, but each of us intend writing to both of them when we get home telling them of our arrival there and rethanking them. We want also to send a box of cigars to a half breed named Chas. Lozon who helped us right the boat after the capsize and get her in shape again. He would not take any money for it as he said, "I enquire about you. You not rich, you nothing but a sailor boy. You need all your money. I get it out of de next man." True Indian principle, I think. I can tell you we are . . . . in earnest. I sometimes think it is too much of a good thing and will be glad to get home where I can *rest*. You see we have not had all our luxuries, oil stoves, frying pan, cover for the rains, and we only have two blankets between three of us and the nights are cold. But yet I wouldn't miss it. I am including a piece of balsam for you.

Dear Father

We nearly live on fish here with mostly pike. They are much more gamey catching than perch. I wish now I had some of your asbestos. There is a fine spring about one-fourth of a mile from here and we have had water so cold that it makes your head ache to drink too much of it at a time. Gracious, but a trip like this is hard on your clothes. I will be glad to get home and get on some decent togs. Don't be shocked at the way I come to table or at my table manners as I guess I would shock even you now. People may talk of the coldness of the world but I think it has been very kind to us in our misfortunes. I may get over that feeling when I get into Congress or the insurance business. The Rowena got her . . . . smashed during the capsize and is not so handsome as she was but can be easily repaired. I suppose you are about as busy as you know how to be just now. Just think that might have been our section of town as well as not.* Wouldn't it be awful to come home from a pleasure trip to. I suppose some people were away on a pleasure trip and did come home to it. What may happen before we get home we don't know as we won't hear from you. Well I'm looking on the worst side and must stop. The boys have just gone after raspberries to leave me to write and get supper.

*Referring to the Bay City fire of 1892.

Dear Brother

I hope Papa keeps you in racing trim with that dandy racer of yours. I suppose if you have a practice course of your own you can spend 2 or 3 hours a day on it. If you want to beat in all the races you enter don't on any consideration stop practicing on your new racer not even when I get home. I am sorry it is not a tandem but then when you are away maybe you will let me try it once around even though it would get the machinery out of order. I shouldn't think you could go very fast with an iron tire but I think you could take it all apart and oil it up pretty well. You have cleaned it dozens of times. I thank you very much for the money. I believe I told you in my previous notes, don't mistake me — please not bark notes but postle "cards." I suppose the kodac has been received this time and is now in the hands of the photographers. I hope some of the pictures will be saved. Although I tremble for the whole thing. It is too bad, too bad. I wish all of you could enjoy this beautiful northern country with me. It is simply mag-nificent. Give my love and respects to Dohn. I am sorry you lost so much by the fire but thank your lucky stars that you didn't lose more. We have a fine bed of balsam boughs to sleep on. My it is bliss, but cold, cold bliss, although I don't feel it as much as Jim and George. They sleep with all their clothes and overcoats on and their cold while I sleep in my underclothes, stockings, and vest and am not half so cold as they. I had my doubts about filling up this piece of bark but I have barked right along and have not found it hard one bit and could write more. I wonder if Mr. and Mrs. Leavens are there yet and Miss Lindsay. I am writing to her. I have never asked to be remembered to Miss Lindsay an oversight I did not mean to make. You may remember me to all those men-tioned and to Geo. also and Frank. Hoping Mama has a serv-ant and is not working herself to death I remain with love

Your son and brother
Roy

Found in the fly-leaf of the Bible presented to her daughter, Camilla, on April 6, 1901, her 26th birthday, is the following inscription, presumably composed by Gram:

"Thou must be true thyself, if thou the truth wouldst teach;
Thy soul must overflow, if thou another soul wouldst reach:
It needs the overflowing heart to give the lips full speech.
Think truly, and thy word shall be a fruitful seed:
Live truly and thy life shall be a great and noble creed."

Written in her own hand were the following pieces of poetry found under the attic floorboards eighty-some years later:

The Rescued "Thought"

Down low on the sodden pathway
  With face on the rain-wet leaves,
All bruised and wilted and broken,
  A fallen Pansy grieves.

Dyed with the wine of summer,
  With gold in its velvet heart;
O sad little Thought, for the mildew
  And blight that seem thy part.

Come drink of the dews of reviving,
  Grow fresh and merry and glad;
Then carry thy breath of sunshine
  To the heart of one lonely and sad.

O sweet, glad Thought, in that service
  Thy gold shall be safe from rust,
And thy wine-dyed leaves, little Pansy,
  Not vainly shall pass to dust.

May Stocking Knaggs
Augusta, Me. Oct. 14, 1900

Where is my blue-eyed baby
  With his sweet angel-face
Smiling up at me benignly
  Filling my vision with grace

Grown to a rollicking boyhood
  Gone is the angel quite
Human and earthly his tempers
  Mingled is darkness with light

Wayward, yet loving, his spirit
  And sometimes into his face
Through the day's vexing
  Come glints of experience though baby-grace

Ah well, Time crowns us and robs us
  The joy of today will not stay
And when he is carried to manhood
  Shall I long for the grace of today?

And then perhaps will a day come
  When who looks at his quiet face
Will know the old look has come back again
  With a new-shadowed angel-grace

Will his mother be there to gaze then
  To gaze and to weep in pain
O'er the angel-babe and the rollicking boy
  And the olive that grew in vain?

Ah little we know what the years will bring
  But the mother knows that never
Will the babe return as it leaves her arms
  It is gone with its graces forever.

M.S.K. October 13, 1875

(Found under the floorboards of the attic of the family home
more than 100 years later. Son Walter must have been her
"blue-eyed baby.")

Gram's sister, Dimies Tryphena Stocking, came to visit and met and fell in love with a young lawyer around the corner on Center Street, Charles H. Denison. For some reason, she was always called "Nim". Aunt Nim worked against woman suffrage just as avidly as Gram worked for it. They certainly were independent thinkers.

Descended from the brother of Charles Denison, Frances Davy FitzGerald of Bay City recalls a story Aunt Nim told when she visited Frances' family in Clare, MI when she was a child.

"Cousin" Frances Says:

"One day a letter came from Grandma's sister-in-law in New York City. She was coming on the train to visit Grandma (Sophronia Denison Davy). How startling that news was!

". . . . The house was cleaned from top to bottom. We children were told we must behave. We were always being told not to put our elbows on the table and to sit up straight. But now we were told those things more often. We were told to call the visitor Aunt Clara." (Her "Aunt Clara" was my "Aunt Nim.")

"Finally the big day came and our father met the train with a rig from the livery stable and brought Grandma's sister-in-law to the house. We stood back in awe when first we saw this charming, laughing woman who was only a very few years older than our father. But soon the shyness left us and we became her devoted admirers.

". . . We listened avidly to her stories and this was one of them.

"Aunt Clara maintained quite a household in New York City, also a stable with a pair of high-spirited carriage horses, a carriage and a coachman.

"She was very fond of the Opera and was one of the patrons of the Metropolitan. She had planned to attend one evening and had sent the message out to the coachman to have her carriage at the door at a quarter of eight.

"The style those days was to have fancy beadwork and fringe on evening dresses and, of course, a woman always wore many long petticoats.

"When Aunt Clara went out the front door that evening she was wearing a small shining tiara and a many-beaded blouse. It was warm weather so she was not wearing a coat.

"As the coachman handed her into the carriage she notice that he fumbled and seemed embarrassed about something, but he drew the light robe over her lap, got up onto his seat, and they started rolling down Fifth Avenue.

"After a few blocks he pulled up at the curb, got down from his high seat, came around to the side and in a hesitating, stammering manner said, 'Pardon me, Madame, but didn't you forget to put on all of your dress?'

"Startled Aunt Clara looked down — sure enough, the shimmering beaded skirt that went with the shimmering beaded blouse was not there. She had neglected to put it on.

"Quickly they turned around, went back for the skirt and still got to the Opera on time.

"Aunt Clara laughed merrily as she finished this story."

This story recalls another one told by my Great Aunt Nim. Early in their married life, she and Uncle Charles, though strapped for funds, went for a stroll in downtown Manhattan. As they approached Trinity Church they decided to go in and say a prayer. As they emerged they deposited their last 50-cent piece in the "poor-box."

Dimies Tryphena Stocking Denison and Charles H. Denison,
"Aunt Nim" and "Uncle Carl."

They insisted that from that evening on their fortune
changed for the better. Uncle Charles established the Handy
Thumb to use his invention, the thumb index, patented in
1876, by indexing dictionaries and Bibles for publishers, a
business that flourished long after his death and kept Aunt
Nim an active business woman until she was in her eighties.

"Cousin Frances" says he also helped raise funds in New York for the base of the Statue of Liberty, the statue itself having been presented to the United States by France. As a member of a committee, it was his suggestion to charge 3¢ instead of 2¢ for the daily paper for one day, also to urge each veteran in the state to send in $1. He was a close student of national affairs and was a speaker in every presidential campaign from Lincoln to Roosevelt.

Mother, whose dark brown eyes snapped when she was angry, told us Grandma Knaggs had a temper.

One morning, as a labor of love, she rose early to prepare a special deluxe breakfast for her son, Walter, who was leaving on a trip. During the early morning flurry, he did not think he had time to eat.

So upset was Grandma she dumped his entire plate upside down on the dining room floor.

We always thought this episode was a fine example of self-punishment.

Uncle Roy must have taken after her. While getting breakfast one morning, he started to pour Aunt Mame's coffee.

"Say when," Uncle Roy commanded.

Aunt Mame ignored him and he went on pouring.

Sister Marion must have taken after them. Whenever her family failed to come to the dinner table immediately when called, she threatened to throw the dinner in the sink.

Quirky, aren't we?

Oh once I was a landlord's pet
When I had money to spend
I spent it in drink
And did verily think
It never would come to an end.

And now I have nothing but rags to my back
And shoes that won't hide my toes
The brim of my hat
Goes flip-flap-flap
And the boys tweak my rum-blossom nose.

Oh cracky! Oh dear!
Reximmity blueskin!
The crown of my hat
Goes flip-flap-flap
And the boys tweak my rum-blossom nose.

My great-grandfather, Dr. Charles G. Stocking, told this ditty to his grand-children, including my uncle, Roy S. Knaggs, who taught it to my mother and she taught it to us.

In April of 1883, Gram went to visit her sister and husband in New York City. She kept a daily diary, telling most eloquently of each day's events. So touching was her visit to Bellevue Hospital "where my dearest one lay in the dark days after Libby — watched and tended back to life for the sake of his sacrifice for his country, while his mother's heart bled, far away, in expectant agony. Thank God, oh my heart in your deepest depths, for the outcome. We walked through the male and female and children's wards. Everything was scrupulously neat and the poor sick ones looked as comfortable as they could be made."

"Apr. 24. A great day for New York and Brooklyn opening of the Brooklyn Bridge. . . . We took up a position on Broadway. In due time the streets were cleared and first rode a body of mounted police then a magnificent band followed by the Seventh New York Regiment. Then the President (Chester Arthur) and members of the Cabinet, Governor Cleveland and staff, distinguished citizens, etc.

"We stood on the edge of the curb and Nim and I waved our handkerchiefs. The President turned his dark eyes our way and lifted his hat. He is a very fine-looking man. I was much amused at Nim's comment when we were at lunch that he did not look like a President of the United States. He was handsome but he looked like a ward politician."

When Gram and Uncle Carl decided to cross Brooklyn Bridge the day it opened the crowd was so great they took a carriage across and walked back.

In the flower of their age.
—First Book of Samuel, 2:33

The young people of my father's and mother's families provide their own entertainment on the front steps of the Mac
Lennan home.

MY FATHER'S HOUSE

"Time is. hastening on, and we
What our fathers are shall be
Shadow-shapes of memory."

—Whittier

June 17, 1775 saw the Battle of Bunker Hill and that year Patrick Henry exclaimed his renowned "Give Me Liberty or Give Me Death" speech.

On July 6, 1776 the Declaration of Independence was published and signed Aug. 2 by the members of Congress.

In the period from 1763 to 1775, some 20,000 Highlanders came to America, most of them settling in Canada. My father's grandfather, Murdock MacLennan, and his two brothers, Andrew Jr. and Donald, came to Canada from Tain, Scotland. Andrew Sr. and his wife, Margaret, came later, bringing their sister, Jessica.

Murdock's son, John James, was born in London, Canada, Apr. 9, 1840 and later settled in Port Rowan, Ontario. By that time the Lewis and Clark expedition had explored the West, Audobon had started his scientific study of birds, Congress passed the act prohibiting African slave trade and importation of slaves anywhere in the United States after January 1, 1808, and Robert Fulton's steamboat, the Clermont, had run to Albany from New York. Bananas, oranges, and lemons had entered the American diet.

John James, my grandfather, and his wife, Marion Hornby of Montreal, had five children, James Murdock and William Nelthorpe, both born in Port Rowan, and Alice Marion, Frances Raynes, and Henry Etherington in Vittoria, Ont. My father, Henry (Harry), had lost both parents by the time he was 19.

Our cousin, Hughena MacLennan Gustin of Windsor, took us on a tour of our mutual family origins in Canada. Her father was John, son of Andrew Jr. Her great grandfather on her mother's side was Donald. Doubly related and all very confusing.

She took us first to Simcoe and thence to Vittoria, a small village once the capitol of the "London District." There we found the gravestones of our earliest ancestors in America, Andrew and Margaret, saying they were born in Tain, Scotland.

Our grandfather John was engaged in the timber cutting business, mainly buying and selling properties. In those days Ontario, particularly the lake shore and river areas, provided the world's lumbering centers. The northern white pine was a very desirable building material and it is still considered the finest construction wood.

My Uncle Billy, working for his father, started as a "cruiser," going into new areas, marking timber for cutting and for estimating the value of the stand.

Later, as the most desirable timber stands were cut away from the shores and rivers (water furnishing the cheapest transportation to the east and the world markets) the cutting areas moved westward and Bay City, Michigan, became the next lumber center of the world. So John and his family moved to Bay City in 1869 when the population was about 10,000.

Grandpa MacLennan dealt in pine and hard lumber, with an office in the Payne block in Bay City and another at his yards at Van Buren and First Streets near the Michigan Central Railroad tracks where he occupied about three blocks for his yard and switching facilities. He dealt in wholesale, shipping from three to five million feet of lumber per year. He also was devoted to general farming in Frazer and Garfield Townships.

In a biographical record, Grandpa MacLennan is described as "a sagacious, thrifty and persevering man . . . held in the highest respect for his square dealing with all with whom he comes in contact."

As Oscoda and Cheboygan became the white pine milling centers, Uncle Billy decided to leave Bay City (in 1904) and move to Detroit where he started the City Lumber Company.

His son, Miles, my cousin, says he and his wife, Ethel, once found a town by the name of MacLennan about 30 miles or so north of the Canadian Soo.

Our Aunt Alice like to tell about the rugged life of the ancient highlanders who were our ancestors.

Occasionally when the family was assembled for the dinner meal, a large platter would be borne in and set before the eldest son. It contained nothing but a pair of spurs. This was a "gentle" hint that the larder was bare and that the son was expected to don the spurs and go out and get meat.

If the local hunting was poor, he was expected to sally forth and cut off an animal or two from one of the lowlanders' ample herds of cattle. Yes, we're afraid that some of our illustrious ancestors were cattle thieves, although in those days of "might makes right" it didn't bear the same stigma as it does now.

The MacLennan clan was always closely associated with the Logans, having the same tartan plaid and crest or coat-of-arms. They were located principally near Kintal on the coast directly west of Loch Ness. The clan's origins were Celtic, as were the majority of the Highlanders.

(Incidentally, the bagpipes are thought to be of Irish origin. I was astonished to be met by pipers when we landed in Ireland.)

Our earliest recorded ancestor was one Gilligom, a warrier attached to the Logans. He was killed at the battle of Drumderfit where the Frasers defeated the Logans (sometime in the 1300's). Posthumously a son was born to his widow, who had been captured by the Frasers. The Frasers, it is believed, intentionally broke the child's back to prevent him from ever becoming a warrior. The Frasers also saw that the child was educated into the priesthood. The boy, called Crotar MacGilligom, became a priest, founding a church at Kilmer in Sleat and another at Clenelg. He also carried his clan across to Kintail on the west coast.

Celtic priests were allowed to marry in those days and he had a son named Gille Finnan after the Celtic St. Finnan. The succession became known as the MacLennan clan, from Mac Gill-innan (say it fast), son of Gille Finnan. Evidently spelling was not a forte of the early clansmen. Some records also spell Finnan as Fhinnan.

All my father's siblings eventually moved to Detroit. Dad studied medicine at the Detroit College of Medicine, graduating in 1900. Due to his poor eyesight he was "read" through medical school by his sister, Alice. He had a remarkable memory and was considered an excellent diagnostician.

Family history has it that Dad at 17 ran ahead of the fire that almost destroyed Bay City's South End on July 25, 1892, to warn the occupants of homes in its path. Started by sparks from a tugboat steaming down the river and fanned by strong winds, the fire burned a 45-block area, destroyed more than 230 houses, and 18,000,000 feet of boardwalk, and left 1,300 homeless. Miraculously only one person died in the holocaust.

An unidentified poet wrote:

> *"Trucks, carts, and wagons wildly flew*
> *Some took old goods and left the new*
> *To save life and property our firemen tried,*
> *One burned offering — Jesse Miller died."*

I can remember walking on some of the boardwalks in Bay City, though most of the cedar block streets and board walks were paved by the time I got there (1910 – 1920).

My father's home was "kitty-corner" from my mother's — at the corner of Fifth and N. Sheridan. The highlight of their "hired help" was the bearded lady who left the P. T. Barnum circus to become the family's cook. Her gift for cooking was entirely eclipsed by her hirsute achievements. And many were the extra drinks of water and the extra trips to the cookie jar just to show unbelievers the wonder of the world right in my father's own kitchen! The bearded lady, perhaps believing she might as well get paid as a sideshow attraction, eventually returned to the circus, by a circuitous route, my father said.

Born February 17, 1875, Dad served in the Medical Corps of the U.S. Army with the rank of captain during World War I. He served at Camp Greenleaf, Chickamauga Park, Ga., with Bn. #3, Evacuation Hospital #35, and Camp Hospital #25 in France. He died suddenly April 14, 1924, at 49, of cerebral hemorrhage. The newspaper of the small town we lived in, Bellevue, MI, bore the headline "BELLEVUE'S KINDLY MAN HAS GONE." What finer epitaph could there be!

When I became old enough, I delighted in helping Dad at his office. He set me to filling capsules, cleaning and sterilizing his instruments, and keeping his office neat. I rode with him on his calls, by car in summer, by sleigh in winter snuggled under a big buffalo robe.

When I was tiny I loathed pink pills administered for constipation. So Dad made blue pills just for spoiled me.

Not until I attended my 50th high school class reunion did I learn the true compassion of my father. One of my classmates told me that when his family all came down with the flu, Dad came to their farmhouse to treat them. When he saw how very ill they were, after treating them he went to the barn and did the evening chores. He slept on their living room couch that night and in the morning again did their chores before leaving on his rounds.

"Try getting a doctor to come to your home today, let alone doing any chores," exclaimed my classmate.

Mother guided us bravely through the time Dad served his country in France. The only time I ever saw her weep was when an erroneous United Press dispatch on November 7, 1918 heralded a false Armistice. Kaiser Wilhelm abdicated on November 9 and news of the German surrender reached the U.S. by Associated Press at 3 a.m. November 11. The predawn fire whistles in Bellevue woke us, huge bonfires were lighted, and the whole town gathered at an ox roast to celebrate.

My father's ship, the Leviathan, had left harbor when the news came. It was advised to wait for orders; they came — to proceed to France where Dad stayed a year. Mother could make the ouiji board dance and when we asked when Dad would come home it said July 12. Strangely, he did.

A dream, that after he died, we wished so heartily for our Father's return that finally he was allowed to come back to us, was my experience. But he had changed. He insisted that we sleep on the floor instead of in beds. This seemed odd to us, and we tried to understand. He talked of things not of this earth, and we were bewildered. After he had stayed several days, we decided that he had gone beyond us and should go on to the other world, that we could not keep him tied down to this world when he was ready for things beyond. So he left us and we did not wish again for his return, because his going was right. Had it not been proved so? I don't know how this dream would be interpreted by psychoanalysts; I only know that at the time it came as a comfort.

The Sunday before he died on April 13, 1924, I brought the newspaper office gang to the house on our way back from a day at a maple sugar farm. The gang met the family and we showed them the saw-toothed sword Dad brought back from France, and the "blood" stains on the Indian club, and other family treasures in our efforts to entertain.

In the kitchen Dad and I tried again and again to make enough lemonade to go around with what we had on hand. He poured and repoured, and how we laughed in our efforts to provide enough for all!

Later when we left, I remember waving a gay good-bye to Mother and Dad as they stood together on the porch. Such grand sports. But I wasn't one. For the first time in my life I had left them without kissing them good-bye. I was embarrassed to in front of the gang. It was the last time I left my Father.

The next day at noon I went to the Y cafeteria with the society editor. I ordered my meal, but could not eat, and finally burst into tears. "Why, what is the matter?" my companion said, but I could only shake my head and say, "Something terrible is happening, but I don't know what it is."

That night I had planned, at his invitation, to go with Dad to a concert at the school. At the last minute the flute quartet of which I was a member wanted me to practice with them unexpectedly. I phoned Dad that I couldn't make it.

How often since I regretted that choice, but at the time I did what seemed necessary to do.

At 2 a.m. the next morning my friend-landlady called me, "Your Father, dear." She did not have to tell me. I knew. With one bound I was out of bed grabbing clothes, any clothes. "The doctor will be stopping for you in a few minutes, my dear," said Mrs. Eaton (wife of the doctor who delivered me). "Just wait here."

"Wait — with my Father dying? But the doctor came and we covered the endless miles between city and village.

At our front door a stranger met me and shook my hand, warmly, "Remember, sorrow is selfishness," he said. I nodded, speechless with dread. The doctor went to work, I patted Mother's cheek, and went in to Dad. The doctor needed instruments which were in Dad's office, the key to which was in the pocket on which he lay, with life so far gone as to make a move dangerous.

I ran with all that was in me that night, the family dog racing beside me, to the home of the dentist who shared the office building with Dad. Breathlessly I knocked loudly at his door. The dentist's wife answered, sleepily. Still breathless, I asked for her husband and his key, "Out of town," she said. "Thanks!" I answered and turned and fled back home, sobbing hopelessly and wildly as I ran.

Too late. The operation had already been performed with a substitute instrument, and life had fled. Mechanically, turned to stone, I did the doctor's bidding and called the undertaker.

Of that night, I can remember bending over my Mother as she lay exhausted and stunned on the couch in the living-room; as I tried to put around her a comforting arm, she reached up and held on to my two braids as if from them could flow the strength she needed.

"You must try to understand that he is happy, and we must be, because he is." So she told us, my Mother, whose whole life was bound up in the man who was my Father, the man whose name as a child she had given heroes in all the stories she wrote.

Out in the car — the car which he had driven the day before, I vainly tried to see the ignition through the tears that blinded me when suddenly I came upon his overshoes on the floor of the car.

Another bad moment came when the insurance man asked me to get something from Dad's pocket. I had to search the coat which still held the shape of his body, his kind arms which weren't there, nor, strangely, could never again be there. I never have felt so keenly the near-aliveness of cloth holding the shape now gone, leaving one desperate in the hopelessness of the unattainable.

In those days the body remained at home and the funeral also was held there. The suffocating smell of flowers — will I ever forget it? Would I ever be able to associate flowers with anything but death again? The minister, an old friend of Dad, trying nobly to say the few words that were in a heart too full for speaking. Farmers, business men, patients, friends, too many for the house . . . they streamed out into the yard, but all listened to the words about the man who was the kindly friend to all.

A flag-draped caisson drawn by horses. The rough simplicity of it brought peace to a young girl who wanted above all not to weep, though her jaws ached from it. A windblown cemetery by the river and an open grave. The salute of rifles, a flinching of flesh, the bark of a dog, and a bugle sounding taps which wound out across the hills and back to strangle me. I wavered as the casket sank, but a soldier faced me and I was a soldier's daughter. The few words, dust to dust; and the face and form of someone dear vanished to live again only in the memories of those who loved him.

A little boy among the mourners was heard to say: "They shot my doctor."

Caisson Cadence

A soldier lived, a soldier died,
A soldier's children, we.
"A kindly man," the papers said,
But he was more to me.

He was the doctor, friend, and Dad
Who answered every plea
He was the rudder of my ship,
Which flounders now at sea.

I trembled as the rifles cracked
In last salute at grave
He gave his all and bade his own,
Like soldiers, to be brave.

At taps, across the wind-swept world
The echoed bugle note
Wound out through hills and back again:
My heart was in my throat.

H.M.R. 1924

Penetration

DEATH
  Stilled his heart
  That he might hear
GOD
  More clearly.

H.M.R. 1925

TYME FLYES

"O Caledonia! stern and wild,
Meet nurse for a poetic child!
Land of brown heath and shaggy wood,
Land of the mountain and the flood,
Land of my sires! what mortal hand
Can e'er untie the filial band,
That knits me to thy rugged strand!"

—Scott

"Tyme Flyes" read the sundial in the royal rose garden at Tain, the oldest royal burgh in Scotland dedicated in its 900th year in 1966 by Queen Elizabeth. So Faith and I journeyed there on a Saturday afternoon by local bus from Dornoch, 26 miles away, with a generous box lunch provided for us by the Dornoch hotel as we would miss our usual lunch hour. We ate part of it on the miniature golf course in front of the hotel and carried the rest of it with us. We were hungry again when we arrived in Tain and, spotting the rose garden with its 1066 – 1966 arch, decided to eat there. It was a place of beauty generously supplied with bowered benches but the bees had beaten us there and they vied for our lunch. Faith got hilarious over my cavortings to eat and outfox them, but she finally had to give up her cake to them and I, at least, antics and all, ate mine.

We decided then to tour the town but no sooner reached the street when we were met by a little apple-cheeked man (a Scottish leprechaun), as if by appointment by the queen. He asked us if we would like to see the local museum and we acquiesced, following him and his little dog, Mac, whom he called "Maike." At the museum we introduced ourselves to Miss MacKenzie, the curator, and she was very interested in helping us trace our ancestry. We told her the name of our great grandfather, Andrew MacLennan, and she stepped to a glass bookcase and reached in for an opened book. Glancing at the page, she found Andrew MacLennan listed as the proprietor of a boot and shoe-making business in Tain in 1825! This was positively uncanny, as if they were expecting us.

Miss MacKenzie told us that the person to follow her on duty that afternoon was a descendant of the MacLennans and if we would return later, we could talk to her. We looked around the museum and admired the artefacts and then left to visit St. Funstan's Chapel next door and the graveyard between. The Chapel, too, was 900 years old and without pews or seats of any kind but very well preserved for its age — and shiveringly dank! The windows were especially beautiful, with unusual brown hues not usually seen in church windows. Faith deposited her ungodly gains from the golf course slot machine in the poor box before departing.

In the graveyard we found a tombstone for Margaret MacLennan MacLennan. Thinking this was carrying it a bit too far, we pursued her past. Evidently she had married a Ross, who died, and then married a MacLennan. We took a picture of the tombstone to show our sister Margaret MacLennan King as this was the second time we have found her name on a tombstone, once before in Vittoria, Canada.

Miss MacKenzie in the museum also told us about a retired baker, George MacLennan, age 80, who lived in a housing "scheme" and she gave us directions to get there. Meanwhile the descendant of the Macs came in and she said that a MacLennan was once piper to the Duke of Fyfe and that the name at one time had added to the surname "ina", making it MacLennanina — overdoing it a bit, we thought. We traced our family's beginnings to 1564 when they came to Tain from the Black Isle, an agricultural land between Inverness and Tain where the snow never completely covers the black earth. We bought a book, "History of Tain," to read at our leisure.

After leaving my ailing camera with a mysterious "David" at a local drug store (David never did appear, but he fixed my camera), we tried to find the housing scheme and George. Somehow we were misdirected and it became a nightmare trying to find a winding street that would lead into the high-fenced housing development which we could see but never could find out how to enter.

Frustrated, tired, and hungry again, we decided to recover over tea and our favorite finds from a local bakery. We prowled around Tain some more, getting the feel of this ancient golden-hued burgh by walking on the same streets as had our antecedents, and then took the bus back to Dornoch. Enroute the bus stopped and waited at a railroad station, the driver saying that if the train were late he would not wait. On time it was, and he picked up several passengers at this last jumping-off place.

On the way home we reflected on the good feeling of having visited the Tain of our dreams, till then the unat-TAINable.

"A COUTHY WELCOME" GREETS TRAVELERS TO BRAEMAR HIGHLAND GATHERING

"There is no king who has not had a slave among his ancestors, and no slave who has not had a king among his."
—Helen Keller

Bidding "Highland sons of Highland fathers. Remember the race from which you sprang," the Braemar Royal Highland Society Gathering annually draws Scots and descendants of Scots like a magnet.

Feeling that daughters, too, must answer the ancestral tug, my sister Faith and I left the comparative logistical ease of an organized tour to strike out on our own to go to Braemar, Scotland, scene of the Highland Games for 156 years.

Joining the caravan of cars, buses, pony carts, motorcycles, and bicycles, we rode by local bus along the road from Aberdeen, winding through hill and dale covered with heather both purple and white. The latter grows only in hamlets along the River Dee.

It was a glorious day all around as we passed Balmoral castle, highland home of the British sovereign for over 100 years. Nestled in the glen in a setting of beautiful pines and heathered moor, it surpassed all Disneyland illusions. On a curve of the Dee, swift and shallow, we looked back to admire fully the scene of incomparable beauty.

As we entered the quaint village of Braemar, we could hear the welcome of the highland pipers tuning up for the day's competition.

The ancient highland games take place in a natural amphitheatre in a hollow below the highlands flanked by heather-capped mountains.

Pavilions, both covered and uncovered, surrounded the field. We sat in the overseas uncovered pavilion in the sun and wind and enjoyed the "Indian Summer" weather. We also visited the tent reserved for overseas visitors and posted our home location on the map of the world maintained so that visitors from various parts of the globe could get in touch with each other. There was only one other couple from our State registered in the crowd of 15,000.

The different piper bands appeared separately to cast their ancient spell on spectators, massing at noon — a stirring sight and sound. The highland fling competitions were held all day on the dancing board in one corner of the field. Men, young ladies, boys and girls, all danced with utmost grace the classical highland dances.

Ancient games, including tossing the caber, putting the stone, throwing the hammer, pole vaulting, a tug-of-war, and field and track events offered brawny Scots an opportunity to compete.

Most spectacular is tossing the caber. A massive tree trunk, or pole, is raised to the perpendicular and with his hands placed under the narrow end, the athlete lifts the timber and steadies it against his left shoulder. He has a grip on only about two feet of it with which to control the leverage of the whole. He runs and at top speed comes to a dead stop, exerting every atom of his strength in the toss as the heavy end hits the turf. The ideal toss is the "12 o'clock" throw. The cabers range from 17 ft. 3 in. to 19 ft. 9 in. in length.

The royal family arrived at 3 o'clock in the afternoon, circling the field in their Rolls Royces before entering the royal pavilion over which the Queen Mother's standard was flying that day. Her Majesty the Queen and the Duke of Edinburgh had a prior commitment, so fulfilling the greatly anticipated royal presence at Braemar were the obviously beloved Queen

Mother, the Prince of Wales, Princess Margaret and her two children, Viscount Linley and Lady Sarah-Armstrong-Jones, and the two youngest royal sons, Andrew and Edward.

The Queen Mother wore a pale blue suit and turban, and Princess Margaret and her daughter wore pale yellow. As the games progressed, the royal family moved from the pavilion to the lawn for a better view. Notable by their absences were security officers — no sign of them anywhere.

As the Prince of Wales, young Charley, strode across the field in his kilts, of course, to referee the tug-of-war, he walked with his hands clasped behind his back, looking for all the world just like Philip, his Dad. He spoke quickly to the R.A.F. St. Athan team from Wales, bidding them to win the tug-of-war, and they did, fortunately.

Excitement of the day surged upward with the arrival of royalty and ended our day of days in the land of hills and heather, smart drums and clean pipes, tartans swinging and ribbons flying — a "couthy welcome" to the land of misty isles, the glens and bends. Hail Caledonia! — I always knew that one day we'd be there!

NESSIE QUEST CASTS A SPELL

"More persons, on the whole, are humbugged by believing in nothing, than by believing too much."
—P. T. Barnum

Fiction or fact, the Loch Ness monster enjoys growing popularity as the years go by. Each year hundreds of people make their own expedition in quest of the monster.

My sister Faith and I called upon "Nessie" in her favorite haunt on a Sunday afternoon, taking a local bus from nearby Inverness, Scotland, the city from whence some of our clansmen came.

The spell of the expedition came over me as we passed the weir on the River Ness while on the road between two waters. As we went over a bump I had the distinct impression of passing over at least one of the monster's humps and believed the road itself could be "Nessie."

As we drove along the edge of Loch Ness, the bus driver and the conductress became very agitated over an unusual commotion across the lake. The driver stopped the bus and asked if anyone had field glasses. No one had, but I stepped up front and took a photo with my zoom lense. As the rocking motion and unusual wake turned toward the opposite shore we were more sure that it was a boat — but was it? When the natives became excited, so did we, and the hunt was on.

Many persons have reported sighting the Loch Ness monster, the latest a skin diver. For the past 30 years records of sightings have been kept by the local Inverness Courier, although the Loch Ness Phenomena Investigating Bureau reports data back to the 6th century. We consulted the newspaper's ledger recording all reports and were referred to the Inverness Public Library for their special file which is kept under lock in their archives. I read every newspaper account of the past 30 years with a guard looking over my shoulder.

The monster, mythical or otherwise, is a fey tradition of the highlands and the highlanders are eager to keep it that way. They strive to protect the monster from over-zealous seekers who would like to use knives or explosives. Thirty years ago, a circus proprietor offered 20,000 pounds for its capture. A whiskey firm offered a million pounds for the capture of "LNM" but this kind of effort has been counteracted by Lloyds of London who put up $2.4 million for protection of the mysterious amphibian.

The local conservation officers want to protect the Loch as the inland waterway salmon route to native rivers where the fish reproduce themselves.

Pollution and small submarines are other dangers to the monster. Angus Munro, the bus driver on a later tour trip, told us he had driven a group of German tourists to Loch Ness several years before. The leader of the group was a woman who told them she had been a spy there at Loch Ness during World War II and it was an underwater missile testing site, the unusual activity giving rise to monster rumors.

The monster, according to different theories, may be a large worm, an enormous bearded eel, a giant salamander, a seal (but don't seals bark?), two or more otters, a member of a scattered family of weird marine creatures, or Plesiosaurus of Lemuria, the Lost Continent of the Pacific. An echo sounder recently recorded a large mass, and witnesses say the "beastie" rocks. Some scientists maintain it is a long wave due to undercurrents, giving the impression of a monster. The only dour Scot I met in all of Scotland, the newspaper editor, seemed to lean toward this theory.

A webbed foot was found on the beach in 1937 and is in the possession of an Inverness woman. The foot is said to be four-toed. Spoors found along the shore show the monster to be amphibian in nature. Its lair is thought to be at the west end of the Loch, at Fort Augustus.

Nessie definitely is allergic to the limelight, swims like a dolphin, and enjoys playing cat and mouse. She is reported to be 30 feet long, has from 1 to 7 humps, travels 40 miles an hour, and according to William McKay of Inverness, sculls vigorously with its tail. He thinks the monster takes different shapes when up out of the water and flattens considerably when in motion.

The monster has been described to be of various hues, something not unknown in other aquatic creatures such as the octopus. It usually is described as black or gun metal gray, with a skin like an elephant. However, when frightened it becomes rosy pink, and when confused, mottled.

According to a playlet written by Duncan Ross, "an enquiry," "The Loch Ness Monster," there is a legend that the birds got together and made a big "muckleface" on two deers' antlers mounted on a seal's back. They go down to the sea and each time they come up the birds make a different "muckleface" to scare off hunters and fishermen and make them drop their quarry, thus keeping the birds, fish, and animals safe from predators such as man.

A big game hunter from Central Africa, M. A. Wetherell, found what he purported to be a footprint.

Lily Mac Lennan, our clanswoman, sighted the monster while she was picnicking near Urquhart Castle, its most frequent haunt. We tried to locate her by phone but failed during our one-day stay.

Fancy or fiction, the highlanders don't want their main tourist attraction spoiled. And why should they? We stood on the parapets of Urquhart Castle for several hours, scanning every crest of a wave. One wants to believe what so many sober, respected citizens have seen. What was that over there? There! Can't you see that swish of a jagged tail?

In an exclusive interview with Nessie, the good luck Monster of Loch Ness, this is what she said:

"I am the lone monster of lovely Loch Ness
I change color often, I freely confess.
When submarine missiles in Loch Ness were tested
My peace and contentment were somewhat molested.
If people get rattled and filled with confusion
I become mottled with mixed-up profusion.
I once lived below ancient famed Urquhart Castle
If I cannot return I get in a hassle.
If people get frightened I may become pale
Upon my stomach, just like a whale.
For panicky picnickers I may turn a deep rose
From the point of my tail to the tip of my nose
But mostly I try to do just as I oughter
Like my cousins the seals and second cousin otter.
But if something happens to make me real mad,
I turn into the ancient Mac Lennan clan plaid!
Where am I hiding? Well, I am right here
You see, I'm the road that runs right by the weir
If you run o'er me quickly and feel a big bump
That's not a bump . . . but a hump . . . and a hump!
Deep caves 'neath the Loch are now my sweet home
But I like to camp out and into swamps roam
For thousands of years I have dwelled in these parts
And delight in producing fierce pounding of hearts.
Calm, quiet persons I reward with the sight
Of me prancing and diving to show my delight.
I'd like to be friends with the highlanders here
So if you see me, my friends, just give me a cheer!"

H.M.R. 1971

Gram (May Stocking Knaggs) and the author, Helen Mac Lennan Rambow

LITTLE FUZZY-HEAD

"Memory is more indelible than ink."
—Anita Loos

When I was born June 13, 1906, two months after the San Francisco earthquake — between the City Hall and the Masonic Temple in Battle Creek, MI — Marion took one look at me and wanted them to send me back in exchange for "one with the skin on." My hair was two inches long and she called me "little fuzzy-head."

Born in Bay Mills, MI, "older" Marion was all of three and a half and going to kindergarten. Each morning Mother put her on the street-car and she rode from our apartment to the other end of town, where the conductor carefully escorted her across the street, and reversed the process later in the day. Mother thought she was quite grown up.

What an age, when one could trust a child to a public conveyance!

Trained as a kindergarten teacher in Grand Rapids, Camilla passed on many of her finger-play songs which we, in turn, have passed on to our children.

HICKORY CORNERS

"The pine boughs are singing old songs with new gladness"
—Shelley

We lived in Hickory Corners until I was four. I was too little to go to school but not too young to visit. The boys sat on one side of the room and the girls on the other. Since I wore overalls, I wanted to sit on the boys' side and embarrassed my sister Marion to death. I also was intrigued with the common drinking pail and the collapsible drinking cups. I made at least 20 trips up to the pail and back.

"Many's the time" I stayed home so oldsters could have their first ride in our car, a little red two-seated Buick. One day it became my turn. As Dad passed the schoolhouse during recess, I put my foot on the running board and hung on to the side. We went over a big bump just as we passed the school and I swung out until I was looking where I had been instead of where I was going.

In the emergency, Dad reached out and unceremoniously nabbed me by the seat of my pants and pulled me back in. The impression I tried to make on the children at school back-fired.

To a scary four-year-old, threshing machines were mighty monsters that came on seven-league boots to demolish me. I contemplated with terror their giant tracks whenever I found them in the dusty road.

We picked pea-flowers (some weed with a mealy pea attached) and gobbled them for real in our play. We played "King's Land." "I'm on the King's land. The King's not at home. He has a sore toe and can't stand alone."

We had a faithful horse, Maud, who knew her way up

dell and down dale. She would return home without direction and loved to sail into the barn, carriage and all without getting unhitched.

One Christmas I was elected to speak a piece at the church program. It involved a doll. Mother told me one morning that Santa had come early just for me and I would find what he brought up near the chimney in the attic. Dry-mouthed and throat taut, I climbed the cold stairs alone to find the most beautiful doll in the world leaning against the chimney.

When I was four, I was painfully taught a poem which began "Mister Squirrel went up the tree to bed, A very large hickory nut fell upon his head."

Stage-struck, I stood there.
"Mitter Twirl went up the twee to bed.
"Head."
I tried again. "Mitter Twirl went up the twee to bed.
"Head."
Mortified, Sister Marion snatched me off the stage.

To this day, I cannot recite verse. I remember only the rhyming words.

Sister Margaret was born in Hickory Corners at our farm home, an early American farmhouse. Marion and I sat behind the big black kitchen stove and waited for Aunt Faith, the attending nurse, to bring the red-faced bundle to us. We gravely looked her over, so solemn with our new "responsibility." We were very proud of her.

This particular home of my childhood was to reappear again in my life many years later when I helped arrange an outdoor wedding for a niece in my "second family."

The two eldest siblings welcome their new sister Margaret Frances.

It also was the location of my "case dream" I have had occasionally all my life: a big bear clothed like an engineer chases me in a train engine as I run ahead of it on tracks which go around and around the edge of my bedroom and I never can escape from it.

THREE RIVERS

I never liked to wear mittens. When I was a baby in the carriage my one mission in life was to get them off. The postman, a Mr. Raynes, clucked as he went by. "She'll freeze her little hands," he said, shaking his head.

When I was 10 in Three Rivers I had a long journey each day from first to third ward to school. But I couldn't stand those mittens on a string Mother used to thread through our coats. Ingrate that I was, I'd tuck them up my sleeve and travel bare-handed.

Daily I passed the furriers. One day a man tapped on the window. All the world was my friend, so I turned to see what he wanted.

"Little girl, I want you to have this pair of fur mittens," he said, holding out a handsome pair.

I thanked him and accepted them and wore them proudly, the envy of all children.

Shortly after, we moved from Three Rivers to Bellevue.

There it was a different story. No child there had ever seen mittens like mine. They taunted me from across the street, "Cat's paws, cat's paws" they screeched. I was so embarrassed I never wore them again.

I was always late to school after my long trek there in my early grade school days in Three Rivers. But a kindly janitor kept ringing the bell until I made it each day. I often thought of him in time-clock days. The impersonality of machines!

I made many friends as I trudged the long way to school. There were the Reed boys who were twins and that intrigued me, as I never could tell which was which. A girl I met halfway there always fascinated me as she often fell in an epileptic fit and we would wait, awed and helpless, for her to recover and go on with us. The rest of us would roll our eyes and fall backward too just to see what it was like, but we never could froth at the mouth like she did. Children are wicked wretches.

Aunt Frances takes me "swinging" to the Soo.

Marion and I amused ourselves going snake hunting. She had a long stick with notches for every kill. The lethargic snakes came out of the swamp to sun themselves on rocks and there we would do battle. Our sweet Mother would have turned white sooner than she did if she had been aware of our reptilian preoccupation. She was too busy sewing, canning, cooking.

One of Marion's favorite stunts was to cross the log to Forget-me-not Island. Fraidy-cat, I was hesitant to venture over for fear I would fall in .

This so irked my visiting Aunt Faith, there to stay during the delivery of our new sister, she sent me home to stay in bed the rest of the day.

That was one of two days I spent in bed as punishment during my childhood. My permissive parents never used more than a look or a stern word on me.

The other time was at the Soo where my Aunt Frances took me for the Summer. We went by freighter as she knew the captain personally. I can remember that he built a swing for me on deck and I swung my way up Lake St. Clair and Lake Huron to the Soo.

There we met old family friends, the Lampmans, and Henry and I celebrated our fifth birthdays together at a picnic in the hills at the locks. The following Sunday Aunt Frances wanted me to go to Sunday School with Henry and his sister. I wanted to go with Henry but not his sister so I said I had a sore throat.

"All right," said Aunt Frances, "If you are sick then you must go to bed." And there I lay on that bright Summer's day all day long under a big eiderdown quilt, considering my sins. I can see the quilt's pattern even now.

GROWING UP IN BELLEVUE (1916 – 1924)

"Out of time come gently, Our days, our weeks, our years."
—Anon

> *I begged for raw potato from my Mother*
> *as she'd peel*
> *"Enough," she said, quite firmly, as*
> *she cooked the evening meal*
> *The crispness of those 'taters has not*
> *ever been surpassed*
> *I wish her hands could peel one now*
> *But that's all done and past.*

HMR

We loved to tease Mother. She claimed not to show partiality among us.

Sitting lazily on the front porch on those long, hot summer days of our childhood, sipping lemonade, we would test her.

"If we were all out in a boat and it sank, which one of us would you save?" we'd query.

But Mother was too smart for us. She put us in our places.

"Why, I'd save your Father, of course. Because then I could have more children."

We knew Mother could never save anyone. She had never learned to swim.

Camilla wondered where we got it. But we know — we're a lot like her. Meek and mild on the exterior, but scratch the

Twentieth century Little Women — left to right, Faith, Margaret, Marion, and Helen

surface and you uncover the demon, Determination. Determination to do what we want to do. "Save the surface and you save all," we have often said — too late.

A cross between Whistler's Mother and Mrs. March of "Little Women," Camilla was a beauty in face and stature.

We recall her photograph as a young girl. It is a sweet, demure face untried by time and the tidal impact of four willful daughters.

Twentieth Century Little Women — that was us. Marion was Meg, the oldest of the Little Women, who married her professor and had two children. (She did.) Margaret was Amy, dainty and feminine, a girly-girl, who leaned toward home-making and the art of being a woman. (She definitely has.) Faith was Beth. How I used to worry about her for fear she'd never live to grow up, as Beth didn't, she was so good! (But she did.) Of course, I saw myself as Jo, the harum-scarum tomboy, with a yen for the pen.

Our doctor-father went to France to head a Base Hospital during World War I, finding four exemptions poor excuse to ignore his duty to his country. I recall his terse postal card message to my Mother, re-read and cherished through the years as his answer to his country's call. "This is not the time for personal plans of happiness. Until the world comes to its senses, we have no right to have our own dreams come true." And so "Father March," or "Doctor Mac" went to war.

That left Camilla to keep the home fires burning, which she did in her own gay way. Dubbing herself The Merry Widow, she proceeded to amuse the neighbors, herself, and us with her antics — always unconcerned, whether it was running for a troop train (by mistake), mowing lawns until her face took on an apoplectic purple, or taking part in the heated neighborhood tournaments of quoits.

Life was a struggle, and valiant was the word for Camilla. I've always wished, for instance, that I hated to sew like Camilla did. Faced with the necessity of clothing her reedy, growing-like-a-weedy girls, she dug up from somewhere an ancient dress model, amply deformed 'fore and aft by bosom and bustle.

Undaunted, she saw the need and needed a saw. An unsuspecting neighbor, Mrs. A., dropped in to find her nonchalantly performing an amputation of bust and buttocks. Thinking such a sight too good not to share, she dashed to the home of another neighbor, who happened to be soaking her feet, and said, "Come quick, something dreadful is happening over at Mrs. Mac's." Lifting her skirts, Mrs. B. padded over in her bare feet to see what the excitement was all about, but wouldn't speak to them for two weeks, so irked was she.

Our dresses, school clothes, graduation gowns, and trousseaus all were made on that remodeled model. Aunts and great-aunts contributed out-moded clothing, and Mother snipped and sewed to make lovely things for us. New material was a non-entity. Moth holes were a challenge, usually covered by daisies or rosebuds with ones to match on the opposite side.

The dress model? It reappeared at every white elephant sale for years and years in our village of Bellevue and always brought a laugh or a lifted eyebrow.

Though possessed of little time to spare from her domestic detail, Camilla reluctantly joined The Willing Workers Church Circle when invited. The Circle was asked to prepare a church supper for several hundred persons, which they proceeded to do with their customary graciousness.

All ran smoothly, with the guests well-fed and leaning back in gluttonous self-satisfaction, to listen to the pearls of wisdom about to fall from the lips of the speaker of the evening. The women of the Circle, thinking to whisk the dishes off the table and wash them in a trice, tiptoed in and out. One fateful rattle, and the minister wrathfully shouted, "Will you ladies *please* be quiet?"

After working until they were ready to drop, the women in the kitchen, at first hysterical over the sudden turn of events, lack of gratitude for their efforts, and plain discourtesy, then irked and full of ire and indignation, declared it was the *last* time they would do any such labor of love for *him*!

Swiftly, in meeting, they changed the name of the Circle from The Willing Workers to Grin and Bear It. This happy choice turned their grin to chagrin at the death of a member's mother, when the Circle secretary sat down to enclose a card of condolence to send with the flowers.

After Dad died, following his return from France, Camilla went to work. She turned to the first and nearest opening, which happened to be in a beanery, sorting beans — much to the horror of the city relatives. Blithely, Camilla sorted beans by day, gallantly guarded her brood by night. She kept her co-workers in stitches by her merriment, and once made one of the women laugh so hard she lost her false teeth down the bean chute. Somehow, the manager failed to see the humor in searching for them through an entire carload of beans.

Store clerking, roomers, and at last the township treasurership fed the family income. This last "opportunity" proved to be a great source of worry, as Camilla was utterly inexperienced at finance, and mathematics was not the long suit for any of us. Mother collected thousands, and we "assisted" by checking and rechecking receipts and cash. However, she did very well, bringing forcefully home to us the lesson that we might as well learn to do the difficult things as they were bound to come to us sooner or later.

Camilla loved the stimulation of correspondence courses so in vogue in the 20's. She sent for one memory course and invited the neighborhood ladies over to practice the lessons with her. As I recall, they consisted of memory by association — a game we later played on many a long automobile trip.

The memory lessons went well until one day when Mrs. Mead, an avid participant, suddenly remembered that she had left her iron on. Hurrying home, she found it had burned completely through the ironing board and dropped to the floor.

Later Mother was twitted about leaving her grocery list at home when she went to the store. She asked the good Mrs. Hamilton why she no longer attended and Mrs. H. replied: "So far, I have not had your trouble."

Mother loved games of all kinds — quoits, mah jongg, ouiji, card games, and taught us jacks. She played a wicked game of mumbletepeg. She did it all with zest, still playing parchesi in her 90's, playing against herself when no partner was available.

Buddy, our collie-shepherd, faithfully attended Mother to and from the small town store where she worked. One day, as Camilla appeared at the door to go home, Buddy seemed unable to rise from the sidewalk. Fearing he was hurt or had become paralyzed, she called Faith at home to get our little red wagon and bring it to the store. They tenderly placed Buddy in it and Faith carted him home, gently lifting him up and down at each crossing curb. When she reached home, Buddy nonchalantly stood up, stepped down from the wagon and walked in the house without even a yip of a thank-you for the buggy ride.

Camilla's was a special gift with children. She spent much time with them, playing, reading, singing, or accompanying our musical efforts. She lived life with verve and enticed our interest in all facets of living. I know she made of mine an inquiring mind as I rushed to experience all of life's goodies. We were chronic do-it-yourselfers.

After we were grown and Camilla was widowed, she worked as a substitute mother for girls in two motherless families, became a matron at the Protestant Children's Home in Detroit, and a "rotating" mother at the Children's Village in Redford.

As she grew older, she divided her time in each of our homes during which time we called her *our* rotating mother. There came a time, though, when she longed for a place of her own, so we gathered up her scattered possessions and furnished a small apartment for her around the corner from one of us. She stayed there until felled by a series of strokes.

Camilla possessed the most musical laugh I have ever known. She never lost that most precious of possessions, a sense of humor.

Gramp wanted to name Mother Camilla Urso after a great Italian violinist of the day and learn to play a violin. Mother tried but hated the violin and wanted to play the piano. She also hated her name and changed it to Dimies Camilla. She took up the study of the piano after she was 50 and often played our favorite "Skip" which sent us joyously skipping around the house.

Camilla had a beautiful Roman nose. Referring to her physiognomy, her sisters-in-law dubbed her "Phyzzie" or the Great Stone Face. Her dear "twinnie" brother Roy, however, called her "Miss Blossom." Those two remained close all their lives. Nieces and nephews fondly called her "Cooie."

We never had to blow a shaggy dandelion "beard" off to see if our Mother needed us. Her distinctive undulating siren call could be heard a block away and we came running. She also could whistle through her teeth and yodel, as well as do a neat dramatic faint when acting in home productions.

Camilla did not aspire to great things as did her Mother. She wanted to be a ninny. My very able sister Margaret also insists that is her ambition.

Skipping Stones
(Camilla at 92)

She wears a silver crown
   Upon her head
We hold her hand
All is done . . .
   All is said.
She's won the human race
   With utmost grace
It shows upon her face

Serenely free
  From time-etched trace.
Merry, full of mirth
She walked this earth
And when God willed
That limbs be stilled
She lifted the burden of herself
By playful pretense, mischievously gay:
Each chore became a game to play.

Like dimpled pools
Created by skipping stones
Which widen and meet to form a chain
She gave to others an ever-enlarging love.
She had a special touch with children,
Her own and others
To help them on their way
(Especially those without their mothers).

Deftly and skillfully
She developed the best gifts of each
And through the years
They came to return
Her love and concern,
Bringing to her lingering bedside
Their own gifts of love and devotion.

Though sight faded as she entered
The valley of the shadows,
Her courage and insight deepened
Steadfastly serene, as eternal night befell
She relied on the love of the Father
With knowledge that all would be well.

HMR 1967

Our family arrived in Bellevue, a small town near Battle Creek, MI, on May Day, just a month before I was 11. We were taken to school by our new-found friend across the street.

We were treated to the sight of Maypole dances and a view of the Queen of the May, Barbara Barker, who sat enthroned. She was the most beautiful person I had ever seen, with azure eyes and long chestnut curls. A decade later our paths were to cross again.

The MacLennan girls took to life in Bellevue as if the town were made for our enjoyment and pleasure. I had paper routes both morning and evening, and came to be friends with many of the townspeople.

We were active in sports, Marion and I, with basketball as my forte (jumping center) and Marion as top tennis devotee. We hiked the countryside in summer, skied in winter (I'm sure it was a gentle little hill, but we called it Little Switzerland. Margaret called it Slaughterhouse Hill.) We were Campfire Girls and learned the associated crafts. Certain we were descended from Indian princesses Marion and I learned to roast corn on an open fire and potatoes in a stump. Marion was great at organizing fox and goose chases around the "two-mile" square.

Marion, of course, was in charge when our folks went away. One fine day she had a towel wrapped around her head turban style and cold cream covering her face when she let us draw lots for the Saturday cleaning chores. Just as we got down to our tasks, a young encyclopedia salesman came to call.

He did not give Marion a chance to say she was not the Mrs. Mac to whom he was sent by his landlady to give his first "pitch." Marion dutifully sat and listened, while we decided we'd be her bad kids. We put on our roller skates and zoomed around the kitchen, hit the floor beneath them by loud knocks with a shovel handle from the basement below, and tantalized them by tossing in Mother's fox fur-piece and snaking it back out of the room.

We got to them and he started laughing so hard he could not give his salesman's pitch and they both broke up. She acknowledged that she was not Mrs. Mac Lennan but her daughter.

"Moon, Moon! Bright and shining moon
Won't you please shine down on me!"

Marion's sketch of us as Campfire Girls

Our handsome salesman, a "dapper Dan" from Royal Oak, stayed in town for two months that summer and asked Marion for several tennis dates.

We knew every barn the full length of our street and played and jumped from hay lofts to our hearts' content. One day I decided to try to fly and jumped with an open umbrella from a hay loft to a handy manure pile. I sprained my ankle and couldn't understand why my usually benign Father was a little disgruntled in treating me.

I was an avid reader of Benarr McFadden's "Physical Culture" magazine and greatly admired Annette Kellerman. I had a gym bar in my closet doorway and chinned myself every day. I also had a punching bag in the garage. I aspired to the Body Beautiful, brushing my hair 100 times and "chopping wood" 20 times before hopping into bed at night.

At 13 I had acquired the constant habit of covering my mouth when I smiled, so conscious was I of my crooked teeth. I decided to do something about it. I went to our dentist on my own and he agreed to try to re-align my teeth for the immense sum of $15. I said, "Go ahead," and the braces were attached. It was decidedly uncomfortable at first and I couldn't eat, I thought the braces looked unsightly and resolved to keep my latest project a secret from the family.

The first day or so I made some excuse about not being hungry, and did not appear at the dinner table. I carefully schooled myself not to smile and "got by" principally because the family always accused me of being "English" in my humor anyway, with a delayed time-pin. However, on the third day, Marion asked me to play tennis in the street in front of the house. Engrossed in playing, I forgot about my new braces and flashed a gold smile in the sunshine. Marion stopped dead in her tracks. "Helen, what on earth!"

My efforts to build a body beautiful about this time fell by the wayside on the occasion of my first smoke. We were ice skating on the mill-pond in the dead of winter. It was crisp and cold, and as I skimmed along I saw a man standing near the edge of the pond, smoking a cigarette. In a flash I decided I'd like to try one, and this was my opportunity. I whizzed by him, on impulse, and snatched the cigarette from his astonished face.

I smoked the whole cigarette openly enough, and then immediately suffered intense pangs of remorse, and downright fear that someone would go home and "tell on me" for my dastardly deed.

I went home and up to my "blue room" sanctuary and lovingly fingered all my prized possessions, my collection of dried leaves pressed so carefully, my diary, my beloved flute, and packed a light bag with a few clothes, gazed in loving and lingering farewell about my own dear room now about to be left forever in such sad fashion. I waited until all the family were seated at the table, my greatest punishment, to me, to have to confess in front of my adoring kid sisters, to whom I was supposed to be a shining example!

With my pack on my back, one foot in the door, and sorrow in my heart for the home in which I no longer deserved to dwell, I turned to the family and said, "I have something terrible to tell you! I smoked a cigarette today down on the mill-pond. I know you won't want me any more when you know this, but I wanted to tell you myself first. Good-bye."

In amazement through my tears I heard Camilla say, gently, "Why, we're just glad you told us yourself, Helen. You don't have to run away. We want you to stay." I burst into tears of relief, for I didn't have to leave home to make my way in the cold, cold world after all.

Speaking of running away, each spring my schoolmates and I were attacked severely by rampaging cases of spring fever. One day we played hookey and hiked to Olivet, sadly taking a train back home when it got dark.

Marion made cross-country history when she was told she could not take part in a tennis tournament in another part of the county because she had just been vaccinated.

She disobeyed the school superintendent, who grumbled to Camilla about her incorrigible daughters, borrowed a horse from the local livery stable, and rode, Paul Revere style, to the tournament. They won the doubles that day and she returned in glory, much to the disgust of the superintendent.

Camilla and Harry were the epitomes of good sports. At 12 I bought a paper route. One year Faith decided she, too, would like to have a route, so I delegated one section of my growing one to her.

One night she came home from school and told Mother she had such a lame knee she couldn't possibly deliver her papers. Camilla gallantly slung the bag of papers over her shoulder and marched out, gleefully calling "Pap-e-e-r-r" as she tossed each copy on the porches of astonished customers. She thoroughly enjoyed her afternoon jaunt, only to return home to find little Faith nonchalantly skipping rope.

Camilla and Harry's child rearing policy, if they ever formally expressed it even to themselves, consisted in letting us expand our personalities within the limits of personal safety, letting us learn through the benefit of hard knocks. It seems to me we had a maximum of freedom.

At home our rooms were our castles. My "blue room" was my house of dreams where I kept my secret diary, exercised my musical, physical culture, and inventive desires to the hilt.

Dad even devised a message pulley arrangement to the upstairs window of the house next door from mine when Marion's future husband Roy got pneumonia while living there. Wickedly, Roy and I swapped notes, and if they were to Marion, I always took a chance and censored them even though she said she'd kill me if I did.

Marion was encouraged to express her art to the fullest in her room, and she also decorated the room belonging to the smaller children with Mother Goose and fairy tale illustrations. I have always thought that Marion's room, like Whistler's Peacock Room, should be on display in Washington. On her wall was a garden growing and painted among the blossoms were the words of her favorite poem as an ideal for action forever etched on my mind as it was painted on the wall.

The following is my poem about Marion inspired by her gift of a prism which danced its colors all over the room one day after her death and contains the poem which was her lifetime philosophy:

I See Her Everywhere
(For Marion)

In each jeweled prism shaft her scattered gifts of brightness
   bring glow to the room and make the heart leap up
In patio pattern of Petoskey, in boulder and stone,
   first tasted and tested on the shore
In butterfly wing — elusive beauty adopted as her own
   symbol of vibrant color on the wing
In deep-woods greenery, in hidden wildflower
   waiting to be admired
In blackberry patch, each berry the sunkissed prize, and
   later squatting like a gypsy, gleefully before the witchery
   of a woodfire she stirred jam in a blackened pot,
   capturing the woods-wooed flavor to be imprisoned
   pronto in glass
In bottled beauty of the spectrum-arranged row,
   high on window shelf
In helicopter flight of hummingbird hovering outside her
   door for scarlet nectar
In ceramics where purple and deep-blue of the bay and
   the shape of her chosen peninsula are cherished
In zodiac's intimate incantations of potentials for the future
In medical journal illustrations of first-time surgical
   techniques done in Army Hospital operating room by eye
   so true to mind so keen to hand so sure
In the perfect black-inked library labels so all may see and
   learn
In the fine seam of beauty she sewed the tapestry of life
   with the sewing-bird as her talisman,
   hurrying to preserve for posterity the stars of family
   and country history in quilted form

In camera and sketch she caught the regional architectural
 gingerbread of yesteryear she fancied
 and spanned nostalgic years by garnering
 every covered bridge
In winter, reveling in the snowdrift dinosaur sculptures or
 dainty flower bouquets in snowdrifts, deeply content with
 the utter stillness of the snow, intermittently shaken by
 wild weather
Quick to reach others' interests by eternally sharing her
 own, she became a collector of all God's creation,
 gathering all that deepens the meaning of life . . .
 craftsman in the recurring forms of nature and art . . .
 color, value, shape, and sound.
I think of her as a young girl, a child of nature and
 never far from it
 flashing skate-blade on winter's ice ribbon
 quickening tennis racket in the summer sun
 hastening to tournament by riding horseback cross-
 country
 chanting all of Hiawatha as we washed the dishes
 declaiming the "Message to Garcia"
 while standing on her bed
 Indian-straight, she swiftly walked country road and wood
 as I followed after, Indian file.
 How she loved the pine needle carpet, the friendly
 darkness of the woods
 red-soaked sumac of autumn and magic meadows
 the potato roasted in a stump,
 Indian-chanted corn roast ritual
And on her bedroom wall a garden mural surrounding the
 words of wisdom by Etienne D. Grellet which became
 her lifetime philosophy:
  "I shall pass through this world but once
  If, therefore, there be any kindness I can show
  Or any good I can do
  Let me do it now
  Let me not defer it, nor neglect it

For I shall not pass this way again."
I see her everywhere
For she is there.

HMR   1965

Margaret

Her loving hands keep burnished bright
The home that is her chief delight
As flying fingers knit or sew
She fashions garments row on row
Clean the clothes a-flap in sun
And deftly smooth the iron's run
So blue her eyes and wit so keen
There's lilt in blue decor's clear sheen
Her busy hands keep all things right
And happy home a welcome sight.

Faith

Younger sister
Following after
Full of wit and
Ready laughter
Others faltered
But she heeded,
Serving country's
Call where needed
Roses perfect
Respond to touch
That soothes and heals
Mankind so much
Garden . . . bedside . . .
Golf links . . . travel . . .
Any problem
She'll unravel.

HMR 1967

Lt. Faith A. Mac Lennan, U.S. Army MC WWII, who later became a Major in the U.S. Army Reserve Corps.

My Father was in France when I decided to be a musician. Mother said we couldn't afford to spend much so I looked through the Montgomery-Ward catalog and selected a flute for $9, the cheapest instrument shown. I had never seen a flute nor heard one played. When it arrived I took it out of the sawdust, assembled it and tried to play it from the wrong end.

One day I saw the music professor, John B. Martin, go by our house. I rushed out and asked him if he would show me how to play my flute. He came up on the porch and told me to put tiny pieces of paper on my lower lip and say "tu." Then he had me get a small bottle and learn to blow across

Dad — Henry E. MacLennan, M.D., Capt. MC

it. He said to blow like that and say "tu" over my flute's mouthpiece and I'd be on my way.

Later I studied with him for many years. After he no longer taught in Bellevue, I traveled by bus to Battle Creek for my lessons. I graduated to a fine mellow wooden flute which had belonged to his brother, then to a silver William S. Haynes flute which I purchased for $180 with my paper route money. That same flute was appraised 50 years later for several thousand dollars. Many young people have learned to play on it.

One Saturday I decided to ride my bicycle to Battle Creek to take my lesson and save my bus fare. It was 13 miles there and after three flights up to the professor's studio I was exhausted. As I took my lesson, Prof. Martin said, "Helen, what is the matter with you today — you are so *languid.*" I told him how I got there and he shook his head and said, with eyes twinkling, his usual "So, so."

I was so hungry I spent 80 cents for my lunch, a great deal in those days, and 30 cents more than my bus fare. I was too tired to ride back home so I took the train and checked my bike. All told, it was an expensive day and I learned two lessons for one.

The "Girls' Six" orchestra was organized, composed of two cellists, two violinists, a pianist, and my flute. We played at family reunions and other gatherings and were certain we were destined to take to the road as Chatauqua players when we became "that good."

Later I played with the Battle Creek Symphony, the Kalamazoo Symphony, and for movie theaters in both cities in the days of silent film for such pictures as "The Birth of the Nation" and "The Hunchback of Notre Dame." I also was a member of the Battle Creek Flute Quartet, a serious foursome indulging in some great harmony.

Years later, when grown and married and with a home of my own, I chanced to be riding on a street-car in Detroit when I spied dear old Professor Martin standing in a safety zone. I hopped off at the next stop and raced back the two blocks and breathlessly invited him home to dinner. He came and insisted upon getting out my old flute, oiled and cleaned it, and gave me a lesson — just like old times.

John B. Martin, a stalwart of the old school, lived to be 80-plus and died a few days before a huge testimonial dinner was planned in tribute by all his former pupils and fellow townsmen. He was the founder and conductor of the oldest voluntary symphony orchestra in the country, the Battle Creek Symphony Orchestra. He was to his students a truly "great" teacher.

Memorial Day in a small town was one of the highlights of our life. The parade, the roll of drums and attendant roll call of those gone forever reverberates through the years. One year a fifer could not be found for the fife and drum corps. They came to me, then just 12 and learning to play the flute. "Helen, why don't you be our fifer?"

Of course this was a great opportunity to serve my nation, in my eyes, and I bought a dollar fife and went out to the garage to practice. I learned to play it all right, but alas, I could not trust my memory of the music.

How to carry the music and learn to march as I played was really a problem. However, I had seen lyres, or miniature music racks, attached to the instruments of other players. Why not invent one for mine? I went to the hardware store and hunted until I found some pliable copper wire, in vain trying to explain my intentions to the hardware man, who only scratched his head at my newest exploit. Very seriously, I bought my wire and went home to ponder the situation.

First I made a circle that hung around my neck, then fixed an extension to the elbow where I bent the wire, which was steadied by my elbow, and attached it to my wrist. To this I affixed an ordinary music lyre at elbow's bend, so that when I crooked my elbow and held my fife in position the music was exactly before my eyes, and at the proper distance.

With this contraption, I practiced marching in an open field so uneven ground would not disturb my fifer's shrill notes.

Around and around the field we went, the bass drummer, the snare drummer, and I. Each piece of stubble, hummock, swell and valley were major threats to smooth playing and "keeping it on the chin."

I am sure that the Spirit of '76 marched with us that Memorial Day, as flags waving, veterans and children behind us, our mounted escorts ahead, we played the martial strains.

I was proud, but partially wounded, when the Memorial Day Committee came to me afterward and proffered an envelope containing five dollars. I wished afterwards that I had sternly refused such pay for serving my country, but alas, five dollars was a lot of money to a little girl, and I accepted it.

Contrary to the opinion of many people, a small town is always full of excitement.

I always attended fires as a matter of course. The fascination of the fire engine one day overwhelmed me. Just as I came abreast the Fire Department door, an alarm sounded and the engine came gliding out in front of me. There it was, an irresistible temptation! Before I knew it, I grabbed the rear bar and climbed on. Once on, the firemen didn't have the heart to shoo me off, nor did they want to take time to stop, and only shouted, "Bend your knees, sister, at bumps, and hang on tight!"

With sirens screeching and the throttle wide open, a red streak screamed past our house on its way to the fire, a blue blur in braids desperately hanging on behind. Imagine my Mother's astonishment as she stepped to the front door to see where the fire was, only to see her second daughter part of the clang and clatter as it rushed by.

"Our Town" was going to have a hard times party at the "Opry House." Never allowed to go to public dances, I begged to go to this one, "Just for once, *please*." Mother and Dad finally gave in, and little Helen went to work.

Hard Times party? That meant just one thing to literal me — a barrel. I went to the grocery store and begged them for an old barrel, any old one they didn't need. Amused, they gave me a lovely big new one, almost as high as my shoulders. I rolled it all the way home, unmindful of observers. Once home, I found old pieces of belting, and nailed them on as shoulder straps. Next I donned my bathing suit, climbed into the barrel and waddled off down the street to the dance.

Why didn't my wan but tolerantly smiling parents stop me? I have often asked them this question. "Oh, we thought it was harmless enough, if it provided you with some fun," they explained.

Very seriously, I tried to dance the evening away inside my barrel, which got heavier and heavier as the evening wore on. I couldn't sit down all evening, but when the grand march came around, I won a prize for the most novel costume. They tell me my barrel made town history.

We never locked our doors in Bellevue and never were troubled by prowlers.

But tramps were a different matter. They must have marked our house, we children said, searching diligently for such, as they appeared quite frequently, always at the back door, asking for a handout.

Mother, so compassionate, never failed to feed them because her Mother did before her. She always felt embarrassed for them that they had to ask for food.

Dad often was paid by his patients in provender. We often were sent to our "Michigan basement" for the vegetables stored there as well as the eggs kept in tall crocks of waterglass. Butter, of course, was brought in crocks and milk delivered could be skimmed on the spot for whipping cream. I can remember Dad once "smoking" our own bacon in a shed on the back of our lot.

We had more books in our house than the public library at that time, many of them stacked in the upper hallway and down the stairway. This caused us to take our time coming down stairs as we lingered to read "The White Slave Traffic Among Young Girls" and "Sex Searchlights" which we thought were off limits. Many adult friends tell us they whetted their first appetite for reading from our quite profuse and varied volumes. We also found our "solitary confinement" punishments (going to our rooms) softened by the opportunity to grab reading material on the way. I read, for instance, the full 4-volume set on the Life of Lincoln and had a complete set of O. Henry which today would bring a pretty penny.

CHRISTMAS AT OUR HOUSE

"Life is like an onion: you peel it off one layer at a time,
and sometimes you weep."

— *Carl Sandburg*

A Christmas tree was not in our tradition. Not until we were grown and in our own houses did any of us have a tree at yuletide.

We hung up our socks. With much to-do, the six of us cinched a special place as our own. Mine was the piano stool.

Gifts were simple. The big find in our sock was an orange and some Brazil nuts.

We hung our socks with the excitement of anticipation. After we were asleep, Mother and Dad filled them with the simple gifts designed for each one and by us for each other. We were permitted to have one, and only one, for early opening in the morning. We begged for this great privilege, not realizing we were making it possible for a weary Camilla and Harry to sleep a little longer in the morning. We usually received books, which delighted and delayed us.

We awakened early for this greatest of days. We cherished the belief that all was the work of Santa Claus long after we were disillusioned. In fact, a ditch digger told me the bitter truth when I was five years old. "Little girl, I'll bet you even believe in Santa Claus, don't you?" he taunted. I reported what he said to Mother, who said, "We are *all* the spirit of Santa Claus, the spirit of giving."

One Christmas we came nearest to believing. The plaster in the upstairs hall fell during the night before Christmas and Mother told us he landed by airplane — too hard on the roof.

Uncle Jim, Dad's unmarried brother, always came on the holidays. That meant a special bird, either duck or goose, for dinner — and limburger cheese and Bermuda onion sandwiches for snacks.

Enough to set the taste buds on end!

WEDDINGS

*"Marriage is something special. I guess you have
to deserve it."*
— *Clifford Odets*

Our family weddings were just that. Camilla and Harry
set the precedent, going hand in hand to the neighbors to
invite them to their simple home ceremony. History has it that
Camilla wore beautiful black silk stockings on their honeymoon, and they "crocked," leaving her with orange legs, or
"limbs" as they were called in her day, for the remainder of
the trip.

Eighty-some years after their wedding we discovered an
account of their wedding done in the newspaper style of the
day to tell all:

A very quiet but pretty home wedding was solemnized
on Wednesday evening at 8 o'clock at the residence of
Mr. and Mrs. J. W. Knaggs, on Sheridan street, when
their eldest daughter, Dimies Camilla, was united in marriage to Dr. Henry Etherington MacLennan, of Bay Mills,
Mich. The house was beautifully decorated with a profusion of wild smilax, and pink and white carnations and
roses. At promptly 8 o'clock, to the music of the Loh-
engrin wedding march, played by Miss Leta Andrews,
the wedding party made its appearance. Miss Alice Gustin and Miss Frances McLennan, of Detroit, stretched ribbons from the stairway to the corner of the parlor, where
the ceremony was performed. The Rev. A. Watkins, of
Trinity church, came first, and was followed by the groom.
The maid of honor, Miss Mary Knaggs, dressed in white
organdie over pink, and carrying pink carnations, came
next. The bride, beautifully and daintily dressed in white
batiste, with a large bouquet of bride's roses on her arm,
came last. During the performance of the ceremony the
bride and groom stood beneath a wedding bell entirely
made of white roses. After the impressive service had

Camilla

Harry

been performed, the young couple received the heartfelt congratulations of the friends and relatives who were present, and then repaired to the dining room, where delicious refreshments were served. They left on a late train for Bay Mills, where they will reside.

Comrade and I

A dip and a glide
A pull and a slide
Silent and swift
Thru still waters drift
Singing a song
As we paddle along,
Comrade and I.

A long and steady stride
Walking close side by side
O'er woodland and brake
By river and lake
In any old weather
We both tramp together,
Comrade and I.

A spring and a flash
A slim body's splash
A swift powerful stroke
Both lithe as the oak
And limber of limb
Together we swim,
Comrade and I.

Days may be chilly
Skies may be gray
Still both our hearts
Are happy and gay
May we e'er keep
The sweet friendship we reap,
Comrade and I.

Marion MacLennan

Marion and Roy, high school and college sweethearts, decided that they, too, would be wed at home and romantically chose the first day of Spring. Marion insisted that Mother play The Priest's War March as her wedding music, and Roy's Father, a Methodist minister, was to perform the ceremony. However, Roy's father forgot his spectacles and borrowing Mother's, he began to read the ceremony which, though he knew it by heart, must by custom be read.

In the confusion and excitement of marrying his own son "off," he could not remember it anyway. He would read

Marion and Roy Lahr

a few words, and then the glasses zipped off his nose back to their button. Snatching them again to his nose, he jerked out the usually sonorously spoken phrases. We all wanted to cry, and so, instead nervously giggled.

Marion said the chief thing she remembered about her wedding was the town marshal pacing up and down in front of the house all during the ceremony, just why, we'll never know. Camilla finally covered all our confusion with the crashing, stately War March from Athalia.

Margaret and Charles, sweethearts since she was twelve, married young. They asked me to be a witness and after Camilla had made a garden corsage for the bride and kissed her blessing, we drove out to the farm home of the retired minister, who was an old friend of Charles', and who had agreed to perform the ceremony at the specified time, five o'clock in the afternoon.

Charles and Margaret King

When we got there, the minister was still out in the fields. His wife called him in via the dinner bell, and he then had to bathe and change his clothes.

While we rather impatiently and hungrily waited, the minister's wife entertained us with tales of all their hardships through the years and all the dreadful illnesses of their seven children, including one terrible brain tumor. Margaret's face got longer and longer, Charles' more solemn, as they politely listened.

Finally the minister came in and began looking for the prayer book. We helpfully joined in the search. I held one up and he said, "No, that's the buryin' book. I use one for the buryin' book and one for the marryin' book." By that time we were all crawling around on hands and knees under the melodian and behind it, at last coming up with the "marryin' book."

Marion's husband Roy never did anything without first getting directions from her. They stopped at a grocery store one day and Marion said, "Roy, see if they have any whole wheat bread."

Roy dutifully went in and returned to the car and said, "Yes."

That was his idea of humor, never mind that it entailed another trip into the store to get the bread.

When they were building a new home at Old Mission, MI, they drove there every weekend from Battle Creek to work on it.

"Five hundred miles to drive one nail," Roy said.

Marion always took the weekend food with them. One weekend neighbors accompanied them. When it came time to get dinner, Marion couldn't find the sack containing the "makings" for salad.

"Roy, where did you put that sack I left in the "cold" room?"

"Why, I just buried the garbage," said he.

"Well, you can just unbury it," said she.

So he dug up the salad sack and they had salad for dinner.

When Roy went to the theater he needed a string tied to his chair so he could find his way back at intermission. He was always getting lost.

He had to "go ducky" in the Upper Peninsula before crossing the Straits to the Lower Peninsula while on one famous camping trip.

Another man in the party, my un-literary literal second husband, said that anatomically speaking, no man can go ducky in any but the lower peninsula.

The cars lined up, in the old days, for a two-hour wait to cross the Straits by ferry. The lines arranged and re-arranged themselves as the boats came to take on a new load.

When Roy came back he couldn't find his car anywhere. He ran up and down the lines looking.

When their turn came near to boarding the boat, Marion began looking for Roy. She posted herself at the men's toilet, watching for him to appear but he never did.

So she re-entered the car and they crossed the Straits, thinking Roy may have done likewise.

He had.

As their boat disembarked, there was Roy watching the cars as they passed, his head turning constantly back and forth like an observer at a tennis match. Uncoated, he nearly froze in the stiff wind.

But they found him. The first thing he said to Marion was, "Where have you been?"

What people miss today by crossing by the bridge!

Cherry Chersonese

Burgeoning branches bend toward ground
Urgent errand — Old Mission-bound
Free the drive up sky-reach way
(Winding shore roads bid some stray)

Crimson orchards, ancient earth
Busy pickers pluck their worth
Ripened summer takes her ease . . .
The finger trails between two seas.

Old Mission Peninsula 1964

Michigan's Big Bridge

Since glacial press her searching hand
Has sought to make of two one land
From shore to shore the span of steel
Now leaps the Straits to make them feel
As one . . . so both can reach and touch
The land admired and loved so much.

The conqueror of time and space,
Big Mac combines both strength and grace
In five-mile stretch of steel and lace . . .
A ribbon bridge to quick embrace.

Fulfilment of an early dream,
Men move across in steady stream
And newly treasured oneness feel
As traffic passes wheel on wheel
*   . . . The Indian drum*
*   Beats through the hum . . .*
Of jeweled harp for Bunyan's strum.

A wagon-track, corduroy, concrete
All led where water highways meet
Explorer, trader, pioneer,

Tall men stood still and waited here
. . . Mac links the land
Melds heart and hand . . .
Mechanic's hand and timber heart
No longer stay a space apart.

H. M. R.

Michael and I were married "between editions" of the Bellevue Gazette, a weekly newspaper I edited. He could use his family's railroad pass one last time so he chose to be married in New York City. "Tsk, tsk," clucked his grandmother, "Married in a suitcase, you'll live in a suitcase."

Our bridesmaid was living in Greenwich Village and our best man was a pharmacist in St. Vincent's Hospital there.

Hand in hand, with letters from our parish priests in our pockets, we went searching for a church in which English was spoken. Finally, our best man suggested the chapel at St. Vincent's Hospital. No one had ever been married there before, he said, and a priest-patient would perform the ceremony.

It was Easter Monday and the Easter flowers were still on the altar. A carpenter working in the balcony stopped pounding long enough for our vows. A carpenter — a fitting touch — we felt. Several nuns looked on as we spoke the precious words of commitment. We honeymooned in Greenwich Village, where no one ever bothered to get married.

I had planned to announce it in my own newspaper when I returned home but was astonished to find it had already been published in the Battle Creek paper, picked up by wire service.

Scooped!

Just This Way, Dear

Are you tired, poplar tree?
As we lean here lovingly
Together below brow of hill,
You lean, too, against the rill,
As if to seek a lover's breast,
Where, whispering, you'd be caressed.

Trees, not always staunch and strong,
Must have moments when they long
To lean against another tree
Just this way, dear . . . lovingly.

H. M. R.

It's odd how you only remember the good things when a marriage does not work out.

Michael and I finally made it to an electric refrigerator after we bought our little house in Grosse Pointe Village.

Our last day with the old ice box finally came and we went for that final block of ice. Michael, as was his wont, wore his raincoat backwards for the slippery task.

Placing the ice on the front fender we proceeded up Kercheval Avenue. Just as we got smack in the middle of traffic, the ice fell off and the car ran over it, leaving us stuck in midair until it melted.

Christmases were always special. All Michael said he wanted was something to sculpture with.

To me that meant only the best — Pewabic pottery clay to surprise him.

At the time we lived opposite Palmer Park off North Woodward in Detroit, which meant a long streetcar ride down Woodward and out East Jefferson, as we had no car.

I purchased a pailful of Pewabic clay, hoisting it on and off the streetcars. Of course, to everyone else it appeared I was cuckoo enough to carry a pail of mud in dead winter. When I reached our stop, I went up our alley.

Michael, the art angel of Michigan, sculpted many lovely things out of that clay. My mud-slinging was worth it. He later became known as Michigan's Evangelist of Art.

Phantom Pain

Divorce, they say, is psychic amputation,
A thing far worse than honored death;
Remembrance of our happiness together
Brings phantom pain and quickdrawn breath.

H. M. R.

MEMORIES OF A PAPER GIRL "RETIRING" AT 16 (1922)

"Imagination cannot keep up with the fantastic daily realities."

— Eric Sevareid

Paper Girl

For four years, almost five, I have delivered papers daily, rain or shine. The weather has never stopped me. I have waded through deep snow, walked until I thought my legs would wear out, kept on and on, my hands freezing, the wind so harsh that it whipped tears from my eyes. I have splashed through rain and mud ankle-deep. I have fought my way against the wind through blizzards; the sleet has pelted against my forehead, at first causing a sharp stinging which then subsided into a soothing sensation. I have struggled against the wind when it seemed as if it would pick me up and hurl me to the ground. I have walked miles in drenched clothing — how well I know the feeling of having your shoes filled with water and go squish, squish at every step! I have walked and ridden under the scorching sun, in all kinds and descriptions of weather. And liked it all.

I enjoy my paper route. It gives me time to think. Of course I meet people, and speak, but there are long stretches in which I meet no one and am left alone with my thoughts. It is at this time that I do my clearest thinking. I have this time to make my plans and to think over what has happened during the day and meditate over what is about to happen.

When I first began to deliver papers, the people of the village thought it quite strange for a girl to do. I'll admit it was rather unusual in a small town but I had heard of girls doing it in the cities and I saw no reason why I couldn't do it just as well as a boy.

At first I was "kidded" quite a bit. But when people saw that I really was in earnest, it was no longer a joke. The people of the town became used to it and thought nothing more of it. Visitors would sometimes stare at me as if I were some freak from a museum and buy a paper just to see what I was like. They soon found that I am just like any other girl and not a freak.

People have stopped me and said, "Don't you get sick and tired of delivering papers?" And to this I always answer, "No."

Perhaps it is because I have found romance in even this humble task. Anyway, it is always the way you look at things that makes them appear interesting or not. Of course, I do once in a while wish I did not have papers to deliver when a ball game is scheduled or some other event that I would like very much to attend. And sometimes I do get tired of eternally having to start out. But after I get started, I wonder how I ever could have wished such a thing. It seems to me that no matter how much you like any job, there are always days when it gets tiresome and I expect days like that. But, I notice, if anyone so much as mentions giving up my paper route, I immediately sing another tune.

Work is what you make it. The thing that has made my paper route most interesting is my customers.

Little by little I have learned to know them and a mutual interest has been created. Somehow or other, when I know my customers, I strive harder to learn their wants and to satisfy them. I am more eager to please them if they are my friends. I have tried to make it a point to learn their names and take an interest in them. Interest returns interest.

Through conversations with my customers and visits to their homes on collection days, I have learned much about their family life and their living conditions. Many I have learned to know and they are my friends. I hate to think of not delivering papers any more, because I will not meet these people much after that. However I am 16 now. Soon I shall graduate from high school and start on my job as a reporter for the paper I have delivered so long.

All in all, I take joy in delivering papers because I feel I am doing something worth while. I am giving service to several hundred people every day, to the best of my ability. I am not ashamed of doing this work for I do it honestly and try to do it well. I am giving to my customers the news of the world.

There are customers and customers. Many times I have been called to the phone and conversation similar to the following has taken place. The customer says, "Where is our paper? You didn't leave us one tonight. It isn't on the porch."

"Why, I am quite sure I left one, but I'll bring another right away."

Immediately I carried a second paper to the customer, only to find a paper already on the steps. He just hadn't noticed it!

January. It had snowed, then rained, then frozen, but not hard enough to bear my weight. The thin crust was glazed as smooth as glass. I was delivering to a lonely house near the cemetery, a spooky place at best and much disliked by me. The snow was still falling swiftly and navigation was made more difficult by the slippery crust through which I would break at every step and then have to carefully lift each foot. Suddenly, through the blizzard came a blinding flash. For a moment I was dazed and unable to go on. Soon I recovered myself and went on my way. That was the first time I had ever known lightning to occur in a snowstorm. By the time I had completed my route, I was nearly frozen. My hair was a mass of icicles and each eyelash was laden with a miniature icicle. However, with dry clothes and a warm supper, I soon forgot my queer experience and became lost in the news of my paper.

There are but three parts of my route that I distinctly dislike. One is the aforementioned place near the cemetery, another is in a poorly lighted section of the town where my route takes me past a dark and shadowy barn. I never did like this place and my dislike was increased to actual abhorrence after one night. I have a great imagination. And every time I went past this barn I would look through the door and imagine all sorts of forms and sounds. This particular night was dark and gloomy. It was still winter, but I was riding my wheel to speed up delivery, guiding the bicycle more by touch than by sight, feeling my way carefully along the walk. Suddenly, as I came abreast the barn door, I was startled by the appearance of several men. I was all the more frightened when one of them cried out, "Hello." I fled as fast as my wheel would carry me, delivered the paper, and rounded the corner. I afterward decided that they were probably as startled as I, as I came upon them silently and suddenly.

The other part of my paper route that I do not care much about is located across the railroad tracks. There was a long stretch that took me through a field away from the town and the lights. I could reach this house by going a roundabout way, but this would have taken more time. Anyway, I decided I would not let fear drive me from taking this short cut. One night in particular brings this section of my route to mind.

This night was also dark and rainy. I decided to go to this house first and return towards the town by way of the road. I delivered the paper and started down the road toward the street light which I made my guiding star and goal. The road was muddy and much cut up. I had a hard time trying to keep my rubbers on, for the mud was deep and sticky. The road was bordered on either side by tall grass, which did not make the situation any more pleasant. All at once the street lights went out. I was about half way down the road. By the flashes of lightning — chain lightning, at that — which came at intervals, I made my solitary way. It seemed ages until I got back where the houses were close together again.

There were many places of which I admit I was afraid at first. But I forced myself to always deliver the papers no matter how disagreeable the way or how far the distance. I have made it a point of honor never to leave any customer out as long as there were enough papers and it was not midnight. This service has repaid many times in increasing the number of my customers and friends.

Many times I have become impatient with the manifold demands of a customer. And a few times it seemed as though a customer asked me to do everything for him but read the paper to him.

Many funny things happen, as in any job. What is more humiliating than to have a paper blown out of your hand and as you try to chase it, have it just manage to escape your reach. Another thing that is funny to onlookers is to have your wheel skid and throw the papers on the street. Nothing is more exasperating than to have to pick up these strewn papers and get them sorted out and back into the sack and on the bicycle.

On Sundays sometimes these heavy papers would be sucked under the wheels of a fast passenger train and cut to bits. When this happened, I truly had a day of rest usually begun by a stroll in the woods in the dawn, if the weather permitted, as a substitute for that early morning trek.

It is interesting to note how different people pay their paper bills. Some have the exact change ready and waiting for me every week. God bless these people! They are usually of the considerate and conscientious type. They save me time and trouble and I gladly increase my service to them. (However, I try not to show partiality and try to give the same service to each and every customer no matter how I feel inside.)

There are the busy housewives who never know where they have put their pocketbooks. Although sometimes trying, it is amusing to see these people week after week scramble for their pocketbooks. It is all habit. They could just as easily have one place for their purse.

Then there are the people who wish to pay every week. "It seems so much less then," they say. The majority of my customers prefer to pay this way and I prefer to have them.

And of course there are those who would rather pay once a month and almost always think I charge them too much. But they can figure it out for themselves and I would be glad to have them.

Those who buy extra papers will often want to overpay me but I do not like to have them. I want what I earn and nothing more.

Selling papers at the depot became quite a problem. I finally settled it by fixing the price as follows: Three cents if they got off the train to buy the paper, but five cents if they stayed on and I took the paper to them or handed it to them through the window.

There are also the people who sit and watch for you. These are many times the invalids and elderly people. One does not realize how much the daily smile and wave from the paper "boy" means to them. I have had some who would watch for hours until I came with the paper. I like these people and feel that it is worth while if I can make them a little happier by taking time to wave or say, "Hello." Of course, sometimes, they are really just glad to receive the paper containing the day's news, and not me at all.

There is one other class of customers that has found a way to my heart. These are the people who have a cookie, a piece of cake, an apple, or something else ready for me occasionally. And nothing ever tastes better than these hand-outs to a hungry kid. I do get ravenous sometimes on my long route. On collection nights I have stopped at a hundred homes and smelled the food cooking for a hundred dinners and thought I would starve before I would get through.

There is nothing I like better than to hike for miles in silence and let the rain fall swiftly on my hair and leave it soaking wet. Many times I have started out on my route, worried over some little thing that had become a mountain. After walking in silence, breathing the fresh air and driving my lungs full at every step, my worries become trivial and forgotten with my love and admiration of the world about me. The mountain becomes an ant-hill. Nothing makes me feel bigger, broader, and cleaner than a good driving rain. It just seems to wash all the bad thoughts and troubles away.

I leave my paper route with regret for I have enjoyed it immensely. If this is a sample of the world before me, I have nothing to fear. Besides giving me good health and a little cash, my paper route has given me pleasant memories of four years and more of service to my community, and friends, as well, dozens of them. And that's what counts.

FAMOUS PEOPLE WHO HAVE MET ME

"News is the first rough draft of history."
— *Benjamin Bradlee*

Early in life I acquired a decided literary bent. At the age of 13 I graduated from the University of Hard Knocks: my nose was broken by an extra-thick edition of the Saturday Evening Post. It became at once my bump of ambition and my red badge of courage. My nosing around for a career came to an end. By hook or by crook, I would become a writer.

I have followed my nose ever since. A veritable Harriet Alger, it has led me a life of adventure, from newsboy to editor, only to again turn reporter.

Although that first blow perhaps gave me my nose for news, there were many other things that I had to learn by doing, rather than by being done by. There was, for instance, that term "diffidence" employed in the interview with the editor in his sanctum sanctorum. I was 16 then and my Dad went with me to talk over the job. Today whose father "goes with" on an interview?

"I'm afraid her greatest trouble will be that she's too diffident," said Albert L. Miller, the Big Chief.

"Dad, what's diffidence?" I asked on the way home.

"Look it up," was his answer, but before I could look it up, it was upon me.

I was still a "paper girl" in high school when my first opportunity came. The regular correspondent for the nearby city newspaper fell sick. Someone had to take her place, and in addition to delivering papers, I took on the task of writing some of the more important small town happenings along with the "personal items" so in vogue at the time. I remember when my first line appeared.

"Mr. and Mrs. Thomas Jones spent Sunday in Ceresco."

I thought it was the greatest thing that ever happened. Soon I began trying feature stories in a small way. My work was noticed and I was offered a place on the city staff, the youngest reporter ever to be accepted, an "experiment."

My first assignment was to interview 75 of the leading business men of the city as to how they earned their first money, what they did with it, and what they wanted to be, as boys, when they grew up. It was to be a weekly feature, and the responsibility of it all made it seem a big thing to me. I knew my chance had come, and I wanted to make the most of it.

Scared stiff, I went to these men and stammered the questions in a solemn and staccato voice, "How didja earn your first money? Whatja do with it? Whatja want to be when you grew up?" Anything, to get through with it and get the information.

What a laugh those 75 or more business men must have had at me! I was as green as they grow. I knew absolutely nothing about reporting, except that I had to get the story. . . . There I was, a kid of 16, my hair still hanging wildly down my back, a simple little country bumpkin, who only knew that she wanted desperately to "make good."

A new day in a newspaper office may mean anything, and every morning I entered the place with the distinct thrill and fascination of the unexpected . . .

One morning brought the assignment to board Charles G. Dawes' private car and get a story.

When I reached the car and climbed on, I asked simply, "Please, may I see General Dawes?" With some hesitancy, the railroad porter said, "All right, this way, please," and I followed. The door opened abruptly on a half a dozen military men in the midst of a ham and eggs breakfast, General Dawes among them.

Of course, as soon as I appeared, all six of them stood up, gravely and respectfully waiting. This unexpected move completely flabbergasted me. Not even the power of the press could cover my confusion. I forgot all I had intended to ask.

Brigadier-General George VanHorne Mosely, in command at Camp Custer at the time, then helped me out of my all-too-evident embarrassment by introducing me to General Dawes, who readily agreed to talk right after breakfast. I excused myself and hastily withdrew, feeling conscience-stricken about the cold ham and eggs for the general.

I soon forgot the confusion of the first episode, however, when later Dawes sauntered onto the observation platform and chatted in a friendly way for several minutes, his famous underslung pipe held between his teeth. I stuck around all morning, during which time he did not disappoint me without letting drop a few Hell-'n-Marias to make the interview complete.

It's a great game this newspaper life. In spite of the long hours, the daily drudgery, it has its flashes of adventure, its great moments, when you feel as if you were getting next to the big things of life.

Take for example, C. W. Barron, noted financier and editor and publisher of the Wall Street Journal. He was an immense man — so portly that he had to take a running start when he rose from a chair. On the average of once or twice a year, he visited the famed Battle Creek Sanitarium for several weeks for the prime purpose of losing some of his avoirdupois. He would have succeeded, I believe, if it weren't for the fact that, as he confessed to me in the midst of an interview, with a sly smile and a roguish twinkle, "I sneaked away today and had three banana splits in succession."

Be his appetite and enormity as it was, Barron could talk equally well on the used car market or the profitable breeding of Guernsey cattle. He "knew his stuff" in the financial world. His every word in regard to finances was taken down by his secretary, and the newspaper made an exception to the rule in his case by allowing a proof of his interviews to go to him for an o.k. before publication. His word or opinion had far-reaching influence in financial centers and no chances could be taken.

Barron was always ready to give an interview and extremely generous in giving his time. For him, interviews were a habit, and he could reel off whole "sticks" of copy during one half hour. He would frequently interrupt himself to mention something about his adored grand-daughter or about hurrying to get through in order to see Harold Lloyd in "Safety First."

Always gracious, he took time to ask me about my work and, as we became better acquainted, often spoke to me about going to college, each time advising against it as a sure way to mediocrity. "It will destroy your initiative — keep away," he advised.

One time I had to interview Barron when he was ill. I was ushered into his room to find him propped up in bed, busy with financial reports. He did not need a lap-board, but instead had the papers strewn over his huge, mountainous chest and abdomen. Every few minutes the papers would slide down the other side of the mountain away from him and he would become red-faced and exasperated. But he gave the interview.

I liked to say that when he left town he was so huge he took two planes.

When Pershing came to town and to Camp Custer, it was a big day. Thousands of people met the train to greet "Black Jack." One of those thousands was a young girl reporter proudly wearing her first "press badge," but utterly unable to get anywhere near the great general, or even to get a glimpse of him.

Desperately considering either going over the shoulders of the crowd or by the underground route through the maze of legs, my look of woe must have registered pretty plainly.

Captain Mains, on duty at Custer, came along and hailed me, "What's the matter, sister? Want to see the General? All right, look out, folks," and he picked me up, carried me through the crowd and set me down on the running board of the car in which Pershing sat.

Everything happened so suddenly that when I did have my chance, I didn't know what to say. Frankly, I was scared to death.

But I had to have that story. So I stuck my head in the door of the tonneau and said, weakly, (it was the only thing I could think of) "How do you like Battle Creek?" (He had been there about five minutes.)

"Fine," was his laconic reply.

But I had to have something more than that, and the car was ready to move. I looked at him entreatingly, and he went on, "Tell them I am very glad to get back as I thoroughly enjoyed my previous trip here. I am very eager to see the Camp."

Not much, but it was from the terse and precise Pershing, and I returned to the office with my thank offering, the only personal interview with the distinguished guest of the city in the papers that trip.

And somewhere in my treasures is that first press badge, pinned to it Pershing's lone paragraph.

A thousand lives in one — that is the life of a reporter. One day my assignment would be to cover behind the scenes at the circus and eat with the circus crew amid greasepaint and the smell of "wild" animals. The next I must go up in an airplane and describe how it feels to fly (when the airplane was still a novelty), or visit a prisoner in the House of Correction, or run a railroad engine, put a new touch on the "weather" story, or be locked in jail. I took my work seriously, rode ambulances, police patrols, fire engines — the quickest way to get the story was the best way.

One day late in the afternoon, a suicide-murder report came in. The body of the man was found, but the body of the woman named in the suicide note was missing. Searching parties were organized to scour deserted spots of the city and countryside. A reporter was sent with each group, and at last, the remaining one, little me, was reluctantly, sent out with a unit.

It was dusk and raining. We were in a dark, wooded section near the landmark Sandstone Schoolhouse when the cry went up, "She's found."

They took charge of the body and I hurried to the trusty "puddle-jumper" of a car to rush to the nearest phone with my "scoop" for the forthcoming extra.

The key to the car was missing! My search along the spooky road (how carefully I avoided the actual scene of the murder!) was of course fruitless and I returned to the car. Despairing, I tried a hair pin, then a nail file. It worked. It burned off, but it worked and the car started.

When I reached the office, the story was already being written in relays, and I was assigned to a description of the scene, the "goods" delivered in the nick of time.

The music critic fell and injured herself one morning on her way to interview Geraldine Farrar. I was sent as a substitute — and what a day!

I interviewed the chef, the maid, and the private secretary, but no word from La Farrar herself. "She never gives interviews," the old refrain. I stuck around the greater part of the day, determined not to go back without my story.

That evening during the performance, I posted myself between the stage and her dressing-room. Each time she came out, I would start, "Miss Farrar, tell me —" but not a word. Finally her last song was sung and she came off stage. I stepped forward, my query ready once more. "No!" she shouted. I had one word for a day's work and thought I had failed.

Disconsolate, I returned to the office late that night and sat at my desk. "'Smatter, kid?" asked kindly old Dudley, the police reporter. I told him my story.

"Why, there's your story, kid. Tell how you didn't get the interview." I made front page.

I had to fall back on this scheme once after that — with Liebold, Henry Ford's prime minister, another "wooden Indian." I was tempted to use it again on Sir Robert Bridges, then poet laureate of England. He refused to be interviewed, and, in fact, prided himself on evading wily reporters all over America.

I studied for my interview with him by reading his works and biography and considered myself well-equipped to get my interview only to find him a willful old man, growing childish. He played tag with photographers and amused himself by lolling about the hotel grounds and breaking the rules of the good Dr. Kellogg and his Sanitarium.

That evening at a reception given by college professors of the state, he continued his antics, sitting with feet up in the chair, hugging his knees, buttoning and unbuttoning his vest, as he expounded his poetic theories. His wife conveniently had a headache.

How I wanted to go back and write the truth of that day! But no, several paragraphs of his ideas on free verse constituted the public version of the visit of England's poet laureate. This poet laureate in the flesh came as quite a shock to an awed 17-year-old.

Other celebrities who flocked to the wisdom of Dr. John Harvey Kellogg and to the best medical knowledge of the day turned out to be genial friends.

Among them were Percy Grainger and his poetess-wife; Upton Close (who got his pen name through a mistake when he signed a wire from the front during a battle "Up Close") and his wife, a concert singer; Ben Reitman, erstwhile "king of the hoboes," Theodore Pressor, publisher of the musical journal, "The Etude" and other music; poor, misunderstood Dr. Paul Kammerer of Vienna; Dr. Irving Fisher of Yale University; and the explosive Billy Sunday, who sent the proverbial 49 bottles crashing from the wall and the devil skulking out of town, his tail between his legs.

I haunted the halls of the Sanitarium, my beat, from early morning calisthenics to evening march drills and covered lectures on every subject. The Sanitarium's medical care, beautiful grounds, and gracious interiors invited some of the greatest minds and most gifted people of the time. Even cannibals came from the jungles at Dr. Kellogg's invitation.

In addition to being the medical mentor of his day, Dr. Kellogg was a spectacular PR man. He always wore white, correct foil for his pink skin. He believed in inner as well as outer body cleanliness.

Some days are promises; others only misses. On one of the latter variety, an incident occurred which was tragic for me at the time but at which I have now learned to laugh.

I was given a piece of copy to read and edit. It concerned the organization of an athletic association in one of the big factories of the city. It gave the new officers, the list of committees, and each committee head. One read, "trap-shooting committee, John J. Jones, chairman." " 'Trap-shooting,' " I said to myself, "What on earth is that?" I had heard of crap-shooting, though, so I turned to Dudley, the police reporter, "Dudley, crap-shooting is a game, isn't it?" "Sure, Micky-mick," he answered, and went on working. I changed the 't' to a 'c' and it went out to the hook that way.

Late that afternoon, returning from a round-up of my beat, I found a note on my typewriter with a clipping from that day's paper. It was from the editor.

"This copy change was a serious mistake. Trap-shooting is an ancient sport, the shooting of clay pigeons. Crap-shooting is an entirely different form of athletics. John J. Jones, manager of the American Paper plant is a church elder. The item caused him considerable embarrassment and did the paper injury. Hereafter, if you have any copy changes, you had better ask me."

I tried to assume nonchalance, since all eyes were upon me. I barely reached the door before bursting into tears. I tramped the streets until dark, and considered jumping into the river before I decided to return and face the music. I offered my apology and protested my ignorance of the exact nature of crap-shooting. So evident was my remorse that forgiveness was immediately forthcoming. The sun shone once more.

My downfalls were counterbalanced by my big hours in those first years.

It was the night President Warren Gamaliel Harding died. I was awakened shortly after midnight by the shouts of newsboys in the streets. Their cries of "Extra, extra" acted like a prod from the rear, and I was galvanized into action. I quickly dressed and in spite of the protests of the friends with whom I lived, fled in the direction of the office, which was less than three blocks away.

The business manager delights in relating the story of that night. He says he looked up the street and saw a blue streak come flying toward him, its two long braids flopping after. That blue streak was I, and all the feelings of a Paul Revere surged through me as I ran.

I found but three of the force at the office trying to do the work of the whole staff. Two extras had already been shot through the press and all there was left to do was the putting of the final touches on the third. After the third extra was safely off the press, I transferred my line of action to the business office, where a newly-installed telephone switchboard was located. No one else knew how to operate it except the business manager and he was too busy with the circulation problems. Thanks to previous vacation experience when I was 13, I could take the post.

Anxious queries flooded the office. "What was the extra about? Is it true that Harding is dead?" As I imparted the news of the death of the President of the United States to a startled people, I felt a closer kinship to my countrymen and a greater understanding of history. I was a part of the Nation that night.

The spell of that first extra will never leave me. The regular newsboys could not be aroused, and in desperation, the business manager pressed into service 30 carnival men who were making a stand in the city that week. Until morning these burly and rough show men came in after fresh bundles of papers. It was great sport for them, but their raucous voices shouting the news into the dawn struck terror to more hearts than one.

I stuck to my post until the regular switchboard operator arrived and I was told to go home and get some sleep.

I went home, but not to sleep. Sleep after a night like that? Not I. I returned to cover my beat, only to find on my typewriter another note, this time from the editor-in-chief to the city editor.

"Will you tell the Cub that we're proud of the newspaper spirit she showed in 'sitting in' on the 'extra' situation last night. Of such is the Kingdom of journalism."

Of such is the kingdom of journalism? Yes, of such is the kingdom of heaven — to a cub.

NO, WE ARE NOT ACCIDENT PRONE

"Accidents will occur in the best regulated families."
— Dickens, David Copperfield

No, I did not inherit this tendency from my grandfather, who, when he was 84 and riding his bicycle, collided with an immovable object and received a concussion.

Nor did Mother contribute to this failing when she shimmied under a standing freight car (too long-standing) and came home with a bruised forearm just because she was dared to do so by the brakeman.

Margaret always says I threw her out the upstairs window.

She blamed all her misfortunes in life on this act.

I say I didn't do it. She wanted my pillow and I just let her have it. We were eight and four years old, supposed nappers, though what I was doing as a napper at that late age I'll never know. Quarreling, I guess.

Standing in front of a mosquito netting covered French window which went full length to the floor, little Margaret tugged and pulled and yanked.

Suddenly, I lifted my head. Out she went, pillow and all, a telephone wire breaking her fall. Foresightedly, she landed on the pillow.

My doctor father was seeing a patient at the front of the house. My mother was hanging up clothes in the back yard. I didn't know whether to jump out the window after Margaret or jump the whole flight of stairs to reach her quickly, when she yelled. She was alive!

I have never seen my Dad so pallid, nor my clothesline tangled Mother so horror-stricken as I did that day. My own goose bumps became almost permanent.

Margaret had "only" broken her collar-bone and by the next day I had recovered enough to want to show off her splinted, slinged arm at Sunday School, wretch that I was.

Margaret was always breaking bones after that. Playing on the forbidden lumber yard lumber pile, she was the one whose hand got caught in the shifting lumber.

In later years, she went out on the back stoop to shake a sewing thread strewn tablecloth before dinner and snapped a tibia and wrecked the other leg as well. Now her Charles won't let her flip anything, she is so fragile.

She had an enlarged heart which she said the doctor said was due to a deviated sternum which she believes happened when I "threw her out the window." It's all my fault, she says.

I say, sternumly, that if you must deviate, let it be your sternum.

Besides, I have my own troubles.

Someone once said, gallantly, that if I would have my eyes straightened, a nose job, and a brace job on my teeth I would be a goodlooking woman.

When I was 14 I got my "nose for news" and felt the power of the press.

Camilla kept telling me to go to bed, but, as usual, I was slow about it. I was Night People.

She kept on straightening the living room before retiring. Shortly, I decided to unlace my shoes and obey her. She thought I was mischievously going to untie hers, and just as I was in this undignified position, she decided to spank me full force with a double-thick Saturday Evening Post.

Unfortunately, just then I straightened up.

There was a terrible crack as the bridge of my nose went down. By next morning, my beautiful nose with all its character was swollen and looked terrible.

"What will people think?" moaned Mother, "I've ruined my own child." (Dad was in France, doing his soldier bit; no doctors were available.)

"I'll just tell them I hit it on a Post," I offered graciously.

It took me 40 years to "get even."

That much later in life, our "rotating Mother" came to spend our share of her year. She declined to go for a drive with us one Sunday afternoon. When we got home she was lying on the davenport with her hand over her nose.

"What happened," I asked.

"I hate to tell you," she said.

"You've got to tell us," I insisted, alarmed.

"Well, you returned the favor. You know that rolled up living room rug you stuck on the porch to be picked up? Well, the doorbell rang and I went out to answer it, not looking where I was going. Well . . . ."

Her beautiful "roaming" nose!

When sufficient time had passsed and we could laugh, it became our tit-for-tat tale.

I believe I received the only known dish-cart whiplash injury. On crutches while recovering from a fall down stairs, I was walking through the cafeteria at work one day when I dropped my billfold and coins went scattering over the floor. I awkwardly bent over to recover my money when a dishcart approached from the rear and sent me sprawling.

Years later a Y-Center bus trip from the hinterlands to the Fisher Theater in Detroit took us first to downtown J. L. Hudson's for lunch and shopping. My companion and I zipped to the 13th floor for lunch, after which we decided to go down by escalator which began at the tenth floor.

Since I had worked in advertising there when I was young, I knew the building and suggested that we walk down the stairway to ten.

Wearing tri-focals for the first time, I carefully grasped the bannister. Halfway down my feet skidded off the worn metal stairs and I twisted in my fall, hitting my head on the corner of the square metal newel post at the landing. This sent me sailing to land on my head, which split open like a ripe watermelon.

My friend insisted that I not move until she got help. While waiting for the first aid men to come she said, "Don't you want me to call Hope, your sister in Dearborn?"

"There is no hope," I replied, lying in a pool of blood, "It's Faith and she's in Jamaica."

I was put on an ambulance to be taken to Detroit General Hospital. Suddenly we remembered the 50 ladies waiting for us on the bus to go to the Fisher at 1. "Stop the ambulance," said my friend, as she sighted two of the bus group on the sidewalk. Stop they did, while she told the ladies not to wait for us.

At the hospital a fourth-year intern put 15 stitches in my head.

I asked him his name, which was Scottish. I told him my maiden name and said that my youngest sister and I had gone to Loch Ness in Scotland where I obtained an exclusive interview with the Loch Ness monster. Just then, the doctor turned to the nurse and said, "Check her for concussion."

When I was ready to be discharged, I asked if I could buy a clean hospital gown as I was a mess. They gave me one and we hailed a cab to take us to the Fisher, arriving in time to see the last act. With my top reading "Detroit General Hospital" I was the best-dressed person there.

The name of the play? "Same Time, Next Year."

MY DETROIT

"The boatman reaches the shore partly by pulling and partly by letting go."

— *Tagore*

My love for Detroit one might say is inborn.

My straight-laced French ancestors on my mother's side settled along the river about $2^{1}/_{2}$ miles south of St. Anne's Church. They must have been in dire straits. They named the settlement de Troit.

One hundred and a quarter years later my father graduated from the Detroit College of Medicine. Twenty-nine years after that I graduated from the College of the City of Detroit, later Wayne, and even later Wayne State. Seventy-five years after Dad completed medical school, my young son graduated from the University of Detroit.

My father's family, mainly lumbermen, descended from Canadian lumbermen descended from Scottish-English businessmen via Bay City, also settled in Detroit. Uncle Billy and Uncle Jim operated the City Lumber Company. Uncle Billy lived on Chicago Blvd. just off Woodward. He had a WWI, "Victory Garden" on the corner of Woodward and the Boulevard.

Uncle Jim and his two unmarried sisters, Aunt Alice and Aunt Frances, lived on W. Philadelphia just off Woodward. My mother's brother, Walter, operated the original Physicians and Surgeon's Exchange at their home, 721 W. Pingree Ave. All were natives of Bay City, MI.

I lived in Detroit three times during my lifetime. At age 7, we lived in a row of look-alike houses on Lothrop just off Second. I remember three incidents: When my ear-drum was punctured with my lying ignominiously on the dining-room table; when the chimney of each house fell into the upstairs bedroom window of the next house during a terrific wind-storm; and when I "ran away" to visit my first Punch and Judy puppet show. I didn't "run away", I protested. I knew right where I was.

Arriving in Detroit from my hinterland reporting job at 19 in 1925, intending only to spend the weekend, I stayed four years. Without a cent and six weeks late for school, I had the temerity to present myself to the Registrar at "Old Main", which housed the entire College of the City of Detroit. My earnestness must have impressed "Daddy Baldwin". He not only permitted me to enter; he gave me the job of clerk to the director of the Evening College, a position I held for three years of my four.

I attended school mornings and worked afternoons and evenings until 10 o'clock. I practiced my flute in the turret room of the tower before breakfast and prowled every nook and cranny of the building, collecting attendance sheets from all classrooms, presiding at all paydays. I even knew where the gas-house gang hung out playing pinochle.

I augmented my pay by contingent work at J. L. Hudson's. This meant marking prices on talcum powder cans or whatever. I "baby sat" on weekends, typed theses for PhD-bound professors. For recreation, great treats were the nickel ride on the ferry to Windsor and a Vernor's ginger ale, also a nickel.

I lived with my unmarried uncle and two aunts the first year, during which time they did their best to introduce me to "suitable swains" at the Ingleside Club, where they dined each Thursday. I did not appreciate their attempts to civilize me, but I did enjoy going to St. Paul's Cathedral with Aunt Alice and helping her tie the choir boys' bows. I caught jitneys, those roving automobiles that conveyed you up or down Woodward for five cents, or rode the street car to school.

Modern Madonna

She sat in the crowded street car,
holding him in her arms

I stood just above her,
one hand gripping a strap

As I saw the surge of the sea of life
in the blue of a baby's eyes

The mother gazed from her shabby toes
to my trim shodding

Envy . . . I thought how a tousled head
eased the hurt of living

Resentment . . . I saw it flit over her face
as she caught the names of books

And as she tried to rest her arms from
her precious burden
                                    Mother and Child.

I shifted my load to the other arm
                          Woman with books.

Tea-Time

It's ten o'clock and the old halls are stilled,
And classrooms with ghosts of lectures are filled

Then comes the familiar rumble and roar:
Mary's mop-water wagon trails past the door.

I look up to smile for I know what she'll say,
"And, sure, ye'll be havin' some tea today?"

I nod in response and smack my lips . . .
(We both play the game without any slips)
She lives a life far from show and ease:
And this is her show . . . so I strive to please!

Thus night after night, as the clock strikes ten
The bent figure stops . . . takes her cue again:
She points to the inky mop-water steam,
"See, girlie, its yearnin' for sugar and cream!"

And I look up to smile, for I know what she'll say,
"And, sure ye'll be havin' some tea today?"

I realize now what a sacrifice my aunts made to have me there, even though I paid the huge sum of six dollars a week for "room and board." They gave up their separate bedrooms and shared one so Cousin Dorothy and I could have the other. I learned a lot from Aunt Alice about the correct setting of the dining table, balanced menus, and frugal shopping. She had been a home economics teacher besides being a thrifty Scot.

Aunt Frances was a social worker at one time attached to the Chase Street Settlement House. She took me on a tour of the homes in that area, my first glimpse of real poverty. She later worked for the Grace Episcopal Church and trudged from one end of Highland Park to the other helping people. She at one time was a matron of a children's home in Saginaw. When she left she took with her a little girl born with one arm missing at the elbow. She became her guardian and saw to it that she had every advantage in growing up, music lessons, elocution lessons, etc. Dorothy shared my room and we became fast friends as well as "cousins."

Uncle Jim was jolly and kind. He at one time owned half of what later became Inkster, but lost his real estate holdings during the depression when he could no longer pay the taxes. He died broken-hearted after suffering a stroke.

I have often pondered on the fortunes of my father's family. Each of the five children was left $2,000 upon the early death of their parents. Uncle Billy and Uncle Jim put theirs into lumber and real estate; Aunt Alice invested hers in stocks; Aunt Frances "gave" hers to anyone she saw in need; and Harry, my father, went to medical school.

The City

If the city is indifferent,
It is the indifference
Of the jungle
Its outward insouciance
Is shaken
By the dull and steady
Throbbing,
The threatening
Inner rumble
Of the jungle.

It is alive:
Great green elephants
Go lumbering through its mazes;
Swift armies
Of black ants
Dart down its arteries.

The fumes of gas
The filth of smoke
Are writhing pythons,
Crawling ever up
Around us,
Shuttling out the air
That means life

To those who live
In the city.

Where the civilized
Is said to be,
There is found
The primitive.
For sustenance
We struggle
In the city.

Still groping on his way
Out of the heart
Of darkness,
Man beats the underbrush,
Trying to go through
Instead of up
And over.

The babble of the rabble
Is insistent,
As incessant
As the gibberish of those
Who swung by tails in trees.
And when languor
Turns to anger
And the jungle
Turns to jangle
And men are whirled into
The circus of the world
They get a certain dizziness
(Some people call it business) . . .
Money making monkeys
Out of men.

H.M.R.

Accountant

A book-keeper's job
Dull?
No . . . I am a
Monk
In his monastery,
Painstakingly
Copying my scroll
By hand.
I count not
Columns of figures,
But beads, one by one.
My patience is infinite:
It is as strong and immovable
As the walls
Of my moss-grown cell.

A book-keeper's job
Dull?
No . . . I am a
Monk
In his monastery.

H.M.R.

In my second year in college I wanted to be "on my own." Three other women and I shared an apartment on Prentis St., a few blocks from the college. We ate for $10 a week, each putting $2.50 in the "kitty." Our rent was $60 a month split four ways. We each cooked one week, washed dishes one week, cleaned one week and had one week free of chores.

We soon realized the unsuitability of our abode. The ladies of the evening wore white blouses and black patent leather purses and shoes. We wore glasses and carried books.

Aunt Alice said Prentis Street was once known as Piety Hill. I did not disillusion the elder generation.

My second year completed, I wanted to attend summer school but lacked room rent money. I received a room free for "tending" an elderly resident on Kirby opposite the Public Library. My room was a former storeroom without doors. Hanging beads provided the only door-covering. "My lady" slept by day and wandered by night, opening the ground-floor windows her children admonished me to be sure to lock before retiring. She ran a sewing machine and did her cooking in the kitchen adjacent to my room. She kept me awake and gave me hunger pains. She also frequently parted the "beads" to look in on me.

Her apartment was beautifully furnished with many valuable objets d'art she had collected on her world travels. I felt bound to guard those as well as her safety. She frequently "disappeared" for days at a time. The janitor said she often did this and "not to worry." As Secretary of the English Speaking Union, an organization dedicated to supporting students from Great Britain in American universities, she had invited one young man to visit her and then promptly disappeared on one of her mysterious visits "to the country." I entertained the young man as best I could during the day and stayed with my aunts at night. He must have been surprised with his U.S. reception.

I earned 11 credit hours that summer, spending much of my time researching for a history of women in medicine. If one can feel ambivalent about a life career choice, I felt "trivalent" as I was torn among medicine (to follow my father), pre-school education (to follow my mother who was a kindergarten teacher), and my natural "bent" — journalism.

I quickly ruled out medicine though I loved biology. I was poor in mathematics and chemistry. I eventually obtained my preschool training at the Merrill-Palmer School (originally designed broadly to study the mental and physical development of children). But I always gravitated to my original love of words and the writing thereof.

Why I thought I should graduate in the usual four years I'll never know. I worked eight hours each day, attended school four hours, and studied thereafter, which permitted me on the average of four hours sleep a night. In order to graduate, I was forced to earn 10 hours of credit in biology another summer. I decided to attend the University of Michigan Biological Station at Douglas Lake to earn my science credits. To do so, I used the tuition money I had saved for the first semester of the next year.

Luckily, an evening college student approached me for help in writing an essay for a contest open only to men who had served in the U.S. Military Training Corps at Fort Custer, MI. He had served and I was familiar with the Camp so I wrote his experiences for him. We agreed to split all prizes 50-50. Word reached me at Douglas Lake that he won first prize, a Ford automobile. He kept his word and paid me for my half — which gave me tuition for the next year. He begged me not to tell anyone and though I wanted to shout it from the rooftops I kept silent for his sake.

Oddly enough, one of my cabin-mates and also my bunk-bed-mate turned out to be the gal who was Queen of the May on my first day in Bellevue when I was 10. We became fast friends and later shared an apartment in Detroit. She was still the most beautiful girl of my acquaintance.

That was a wonderful summer spent entirely outdoors. We rose for early birdwatch for Ornithology, chased butterflies and insects for Entomology, and ran a trap-line and hunted snakes for Herpetology. We studied bats first-hand and in the laboratory and collected and dissected to our hearts' content. Lake, rivers, swamps, and woods were our happy habitat. And since our cabins were widely separated from those for men, we skinny-dipped before retiring, making a wild dash for pyjamas and bed. We drew lots for upper and lower berths, as the upper springs shed bits of black metal on the sleeper below, and we would waken to find our faces speckled.

I developed kidney trouble that summer, tho, as I was the only girl in the birdwatching detail that began at 4 a.m. and lasted for hours. I was afraid to lag too far behind the rest and never could find a tree I felt was ample to hide a "pit stop." What a pity, for the more I put off "going" the more urgent it became. It took me months to recover from it.

Back at school in Detroit, I was offered the editorship of The Detroit Collegian, the first woman to be so honored. It was a paid job so for my senior year I gave up my clerk-ship to concentrate on journalism once more. That was a great year and I had much to learn, but the friends I made working on the college paper have remained lifelong. Many became well-known writers, Saul K. Padover, historian, "Happy" Abbott, Paul Lutzeier, Nolan Miller, and John Bailey.

The year I graduated (1929) the stock market collapsed Oct. 29. Lindbergh had soloed his non-stop flight from New York to Paris in 1927. The next year Amelia Earhart became the first woman to fly the Atlantic. The political campaign slogan was "A chicken in every pot, a car in every garage."

Upon graduation I obtained a job as an advertising copywriter with J. L. Hudson in downtown Detroit. I was given three floors of merchandise to cover — rugs, carpeting, and draperies, kitchen and chinaware, and furniture and the "Model Home." One quarter-page newspaper ad for oriental rugs in those days cost $500. I wonder what it would cost today?

Fifty years later I was eating lunch alone on the mezzanine at Hudson's when I overheard two young men at the next table discussing exactly the same problems I had had in writing ads for those departments. I kept a discreet silence but was greatly amused that things had not changed in so many years. Now they have done away with the downtown store. It was one of a kind.

We'd often skip across the street to Saunders' for a quick lunch though you sometimes had to stand two or three deep behind a counter stool. Occasionally now I hear that Saunders contemplates giving up the ghost. I also hear about changes contemplated at the Institute of Art. While in college I often would take my lunch over to watch Diego Reviera paint his wonderful murals of industrial Detroit.

I loved the big double-decker buses that traversed the main thoroughfares of Detroit. I once took an evening college Iranian student on a complete bus tour of the city atop one of the green giants. He had been sent by his government to study the auto industry but remained to become a doctor. He later delivered the first-born son of the Shah and his Empress.

One of the main sights was the immense Detroit Jewel Garland Range which stood on East Jefferson at the foot of Adair for so many years.

Toto

With strange jocundry
And laughter provoking pity
The calliope passes by
A clown of the city

H.M.R.

Concern

Just as the ferries on the river
Try to whistle
Their signals to one another
Only to emit
Hoarse and ghastly
Sounds
So we try to shout
One to the other
Warning signals through life
And always our attempts
Seem to be no more than
Squibs.

SURVIVING THE DEPRESSION

"My days are swifter than a weaver's shuttle."
— Job, IX, 25.

I was married in April 1931 when I returned to the city of Detroit the third time, braving the depths of the depression. The bank panic closed 305 banks in September and 522 by October. The next year the unemployed in the U.S. reached 13,000,000.

Michael worked for the City Welfare Department as a home visitor, literally running from one home to the next as we had no car and his client load was heavy. He said he "heard" a Chinaman's heart break because he had to seek help.

I worked for the Detroit Community Fund assigned as a home visitor for both the LaBelle Street and Cardoni Street Settlement Houses in Highland Park. I walked.

Highland Park throve until 1927 when the last Model T was produced in the "crystal palace" now a registered historic site. The people owned their homes and were thriving until the move to River Rouge where the Model A was introduced in 1928.

As Louis Cook said so sagely, "Auto firms giveth, and auto firms also taketh away." Highland Park was never the same again.

The area was inhabited by a motley group of residents of foreign extraction, including Greek, Turkish, Armenian, Sicilian, Italian, Iranian, Lebanese, and Polish. They were all proud, self-sustaining people until the depression hit. The settlement houses strove to ascertain their needs for food, clothing, and recreation and to fulfill them in some way. My job was home visitation to survey those needs and encourage them to take advantage of help available.

Mama Rankin
Settlement House — 1930

Though death
Took from her
The one who called her "Mother,"
She did not put his things away
And say, "There is no other."
She opened up her arms to them,
Those children of the poor;
Bewildered thousands have by now
Opened wide the door
From decadence and dirt
To worlds unknown before.
They've learned that larger way of living
Through her to whom
Life means one thing
And that one thing is giving.

Challenge
Fresh Air Camp — 1926

"Hands clean, boys, hands clean?"
The cry rings out in the burning sun,
As the spawn of the slums file one by one
Into the mess-hall at noon.

When my soul comes one day
To the mess-hall of fate
May I answer the challenge flung out at the gate:
"Hands clean, Lord, hands clean!"

I at one time lived at the Cardoni Street Settlement House, where recreation at that time was segregated, at least the dances.

When the Detroit Community Fund could no longer pay us in cash, we received scrip. To earn cash for streetcar fare and shoe leather I took my trusty typewriter through the office buildings on Saturdays and typed statements for professional men. I wrote ads for the Brownie Baby Food Co. and typed articles for the American Druggist for an endocrinologist at Parke, Davis and Co. He later led me to a job as secretary to the head of the biological and hospital division at Parke, Davis where I remained for five years.

The National Hospital Day promotion began there and I learned about a new lay position of hospital administrator which I resolved to become.

However I was first to experience working as a medical secretary to the chief of surgery at the University of Michigan which led to a two-year stint as secretary to the chief of pathology at Eloise Hospital, now Wayne County General. Living in Wayne, MI, brought a chance to be administrator of a small private hospital operated by a group of doctors. To prepare for this, I took the only available mini-course in hospital administration offered by the American College of Surgeons at the University of Chicago. This experience later on in life enabled me to become administrator of Presque Isle General Hospital, Presque Isle, Me.

While living in Wayne, my daughter and I were gassed by a defective electric refrigerator and I was admonished to take her to a place where she could breathe salt air or I might lose her.

So off to the Florida coast we went, spending the winter at Pompano Beach. But, alas, the Miami pediatrician said one winter would not do it. So I became an assistant field director for the American Red Cross assigned to the Southeastern Area.

First I had to spend a month in Washington, D.C. in training with 50 men bound mostly for overseas work. The first year I was assigned to the Women's Army Corps at Daytona Beach and the second year with the SPARS at Palm Beach, Fla.

While in Washington I lived in a small residential hotel. One day on the elevator I overheard a woman resident say she had a sprained ankle and wished she could soak it in a tub but all she had in her room was a lavatory. When I reached my room the Red Cross spirit rose and I called her and invited her to soak her injured ankle in my tub.

We became good friends and she invited me to visit her place of work, National Headquarters of the Federation of Women's Clubs.

My last day in Washington I stopped enroute to the depot. She escorted me through the national headquarters and on the stairway landing I saw a photograph of my Great-Aunt Nim! Talk about serendipity! She was at one time President of the national group and represented it in Paris, I learned.

Poise

Just when some
Pegasus thought of mine
Soars to the
Heights
To dwell there
With the gods
And I am filled
With the yeast
Of self-satisfaction,
Then do I hear
From the thickets
Of my heart
A bird sing sweetly,
"Pewee."

H.M.R.

Next I was advised to take my daughter to a dry northern climate before returning to Michigan. The next two years were spent in Maine in the vast Aroostook County potato empire, where they needed someone to head their main hospital. I was told by the conductor on the train enroute there that I would need to wear two layers of winter underwear — one for the cold climate and the other for the cold reception.

Such was not the case. I took the community problems to heart and they made me welcome. They worked out their many problems in the two years I stayed and later built a beautiful new hospital through the generosity of Senator Gould.

I learned to enjoy life in Maine — the picnics on snowshoe, hunting for fiddleheads, the crispness of the deep snow and dry cold. When my daughter turned from the front walk into the road in winter I could no longer see her. That is the land where mailboxes soar to heights in winter. And the long winter nights are dispersed by groups reading aloud the plays on Broadway. Bless the Pierian club. Part of my heart will always remain in Maine.

GOVERNMENT GAL

Then I came full circle and returned to Battle Creek to take up a new life with a second family. I worked first at the Kellogg Foundation, prestigious place with far-reaching programs but I was not busy enough and looked across the street at the overly busy Percy Jones Army Hospital housed in the former Battle Creek Sanitarium. There I felt really needed and worked for six years as secretary to successive chiefs of surgery, administratively responsible for all the ward clerks and secretaries in surgical service.

The thousands of military patients treated there included many amputees and plastic surgery patients requiring multiple operations. The care and speed of paper work often meant how long the patients would have to remain. Morale of the workers was never better. We worked six and seven-day weeks when necessary and any party games always wound up with medical spelldowns "just for fun." The office employees took their work very seriously and forever maintained that working there was the most satisfying employment of their lives.

I felt a little like Walt Whitman and from time to time tried to record in verse the changing feelings of men who had been to war.

The Hospital closed in 1952 and reopened for the wounded of the Korean Conflict in 1953. Frostbite caused the majority of the wounds and amputations sometimes rose to hundreds a month. Toes frequently dropped off while the patients awaited surgery.

In 1954 the Hospital closed and Civil Defense National Headquarters moved in. The revolving door at the Federal Center found me back on the job, this time as a writer for the next eight years. The Defense Logistics Services Center moved in when Civil Defense moved back to Washington, D.C. While waiting out the change-over, the writers were put to the task of answering the hundreds of letters on civil defense written by children to President Kennedy. When DLSC moved in, I went from writing for civil defense to writing for a worldwide publication called Global Disposal devoted to placing surplus government property where it was most needed. One of my first auctions experienced was a $13,000,000 one in Chicago. We covered materiel from buttons to battleships.

Supererogation

"Seven million men by '43"
March into the maw of Mars
No other way will set men free
But to follow the stripes and stars.

No other urge can they obey
As trumpets summon to tireless tramp
Theirs no longer the will to stay
From bivouac in the cold and damp.

Hardened they are, with no complaint
Forward to fight for a spirit free
Ready to give without restraint:
They do this for you, they do it for me.

1942

Conscientious Objector
May 1942

Fanfare of fifers, silence your trill
Your shrill notes are the cry of the kill!
Tho bugles blow, I shall not follow
No act of mine shall mock and hollow
The gloried deeds done "in Thy Name"
For "God With Us" I could not maim,
Nor choose to deal out, swiftly, death

Tho by my choice, in one quick breath
By men on earth I am condemned;
Our way of life not to defend,
Refusing to follow the high command,
Already dead before them I stand.

To die is nothing; to live and then
To lose that elusive essence of men:
A wail from the wilderness, of truth a dream
From fringe to the focus, and to fringe we seem
To be . . . and then not; but, I know, to kill
Forever blots the soul's sweet will.

Tho I be dead in others' eyes
I my Self cannot despise
I do refuse, I cannot choose
To follow, tho bugles blow.

Conscientious Acceptor
August 1942

I have no choice, no still small voice
But thundering thought, all-compelling ought
Yesterday I knew thus-and-thus were so:
Today I know that I must go.

Peace Pilots

Across the broadly stippled sky
A nation's dreams in planes they fly . . .
   In strength to strive for world-wide peace
   And hope for hearts in swift release
   From ways so taut with terror's trend . . .
On wings, to freedom's fort ascend!

Strange, strange the pathway to our fate
   The only means . . . to devastate!
O, war-torn man with blood-filled cup
   Beseech the sky! Look up, look up!

March of the Phantom Feet

Down the corridor they come
Phantom flute and phantom drum
Hear the march of phantom feet,
Feet that now cannot be fleet
Missing hands that can't salute,
Hands that can't play drum or flute
Mute the march on swinging crutch
Faint their sound, their message much
Clear their chant down corridor,
"War no more, oh, NO MORE WAR!"

Percy Jones Army Hospital
Amputee Ward   1953

Vial Upon the Sun

Now Pandora,
Child of the alphabet age,
Fed upon alphabet soup and cereal,
Mushrooming in one decade from
A for atom to
H for hydrogen,
And on to ground zero,
Now the box is opened,
What do you do?

Humanity struggles with its
Giant jack-in-the-box
Too big for its container,
Seeking safe shelter before it is too late
To escape the long trailing finger of fallout
Following bomb bursts at civilization's ground zero.

What are you going to do
Now, Pandora?

After 26 years in government service the time to retire finally came and the old revolving door stood me in good stead as it let me out as well as in. I should really say re-tire, as retirement is a chance for a turn of direction and new interests. Fifty years is long enough to work.

There is never time enough.

> *Time*
> *Steals the pie*
> *In the pantry*
> *While we wait for it*
> *To cool.*

> *HMR.*

The Revolving Door Moves in the Best Circles

> *And now, once more*
> *Revolves the door —*
> *Turnstile to the future.*

> *HMR 1974*

SOURCES OF INFORMATION

Knaggs Family History, edited by Robert B. Ross, published by Clarence M. Burton, Detroit, 1902.

The Stocking Ancestry, comprising the descendants of George Stocking, founder of the American Family; edited and published by the Rev. Charles Henry Wright Stocking, D.D., the Lakeside Press, 1903.

Files of the Michigan State Library, Lansing, MI, containing original articles by May Stocking Knaggs.

Files of the Bay City Times; Michigan Pioneer Collection of 1890

History of Bay County

Women of Bay County, 1809 – 1980, published by the Museum of the Great Lakes, Bay City, MI, 1980.

The Encyclopedia of American Facts and Dates, Gordon Carruth.

The Clans and Tartans of Scotland by Robert Bain.

Findings of Patricia Drury, present owner of "Off Center."

Input of my family, friends, "cousins, and my aunts."